Crisis Intervention Theory and Practice:

A Source Book

By

Larry L. Smith
Graduate School of Social Work
University of Utah

University Press
of America™

TABLE OF CONTENTS

PART III

PRACTICE AREAS OF CRISIS INTERVENTION

CHAPTER

PART IV

TOWARD A MORE GENERAL THEORY OF CRISIS INTERVENTION

CHAPTER

ACKNOWLEDGEMENTS

Appreciation is expressed to Dr. Dean H. Hepworth for the countless hours of assistance he gave the writer in completing this source book. From the beginning of the source book to its completion, Dr. Hepworth has shown an abiding interest and commitment to the manuscript that continually encouraged and sustained the writer. Appreciation is also expressed to Dr. James J. McNamara, Dr. Boyd E. Oviatt, and Gil Meier for the valuable suggestions they gave in improving the final manuscript. Deepest appreciation and love is also extended to the writer's parents, Edward Lorenzo and Mildred Gutke Smith, for the invaluable lessons of life they shared with the writer, especially the desire to always improve one's self.

The purposes of this study on crisis intervention theory and practice were: (1) To review and compare the various conceptual frameworks that have been used to describe crisis intervention; (2) To examine and describe how these various conceptual frameworks of crisis intervention have been operationalized into practice and used with such selected problems of living as marital and family conflicts, emergency hospitalization, suicide, etc.; (3) To analyze the similarities and differences between these various conceptual frameworks and practices of crisis intervention and planned short-term treatment; (4) To develop a general conceptual framework for crisis intervention that can be operationalized into practice across a variety of problem areas. In completing these four research objectives, the study consisted in large part of an exhaustive research and review of the literature on crisis intervention up to and including December of 1972.

The findings of the study revealed that the most notable contributions to the theory and development of crisis intervention were made by the following authors: Erich Lindemann and Gerald Caplan, Lydia Rapoport, Howard J. Parad, Gerald F. Jacobsen, and Donna C. Aguilera. A review of the contributions of these and other crisis theorists indicated that most crisis authors have conceptualized the essential features of the crisis reaction. In fact, most theorists are still using Caplan's earlier definition of a crisis along with his characteristic stages of development. Unfortunately, most crisis theorists were less precise in their conceptualizations of crisis practice. Consequently, it was often difficult to see how crisis theory was operationalized into practice because the treatment models were so vague.

The review of the crisis literature also indicated that crisis practice focuses primarily on the five following areas: (1) childhood and adolescent crises, (2) mental health problems, (3) marital and family conflicts, (4) emergency hospitalization, and (5) suicide prevention. Of these five practice areas, the model of Langsley and Kaplan for families in crisis is probably the most comprehensive conceptualization of crisis treatment. In comparison, most crisis practitioners are still vague in their conceptualizations of treatment models. Therefore, any outcome research conducted by most crisis practitioners is subject to criticism because of the limited conceptualizations of the treatment models being tested.

A comparison of crisis intervention with Reid and Epstein's model of planned short-term treatment (task-centered casework) revealed some important differences. Planned short-term treatment can be adapted to more problems of living than crisis intervention. In addition, planned short-term treatment is a more definitive model of practice than crisis intervention. However, when the individual or family is experiencing a crisis reaction precipitated by a hazardous event or significant loss, crisis intervention remains the accepted treatment of choice.

The study also included a general theory of crisis intervention that can be adapted to a variety of practice settings. This crisis model presents the practitioner with a systematic and descriptive conceptualization of crisis intervention. In addition, the model is designed to help all students of crisis intervention to follow the stages of crisis practice from the initial contact through termination.

Based on the findings of this study, it was concluded that crisis intervention is not yet a definitive model of social intervention. This seems to have occurred because most crisis authors have not operationalized crisis theory into comprehensive treatment plans. One of the best ways to increase the effectiveness of crisis practice is for theorists and practitioners to focus their efforts on conceptualizing crisis treatment. In particular, they need to describe the process of crisis treatment from the initial contact through termination. As this refinement of crisis treatment continues, crisis intervention will more readily be acknowledged as the treatment of choice for individuals and families in crisis.

PART I

INTRODUCTION AND METHODOLOGY

CHAPTER I

INTRODUCTION

A Brief History of Crisis Intervention

According to Howard J. Parad (1971), crisis intervention is
"a process for actively influencing the psychosocial functioning of
individuals during a period of disequilibrium [p. 196]." Morley
(1970, p. 15) believes the first recorded instance of crisis intervention concerned one of Freud's cases which dealt with the treatment
of a famous symphony orchestra conductor, Bruno Walter. In his
autobiography, Walter explained that in 1906 he went to Freud after
developing a partial paralysis in his right arm shortly after the
birth of his first child. Expecting to spend months in deep analysis,
Walter was taken by surprise when Freud's treatment sessions lasted
for only six visits and finally culminated in following Freud's
suggestion of taking a short vacation. After the vacation, Walter had
no further trouble with the partial paralysis. At this point in the
discussion, it is important to note that this brief description of
Freud's limited treatment should not be labeled as a clear example of
crisis intervention. In fact, Morley (1970) underscored this point
by stating that this "intervention would offer an example of brief
treatment, however, and could not truly be considered an example of
modern crisis intervention [p. 15]". Apparently, Morley included this
case study as a pivotal part of the development of crisis intervention

because it illustrated the rapid onset of symptoms along with an abbreviated treatment plan — two characteristics of modern crisis intervention.

Most experts (Aguilera, 1970b; Morley, 1970; Parad, 1971; Rapoport, 1970) have pointed to the pioneering work of Erich Lindemann (1944, 1956, 1965) as the birth of modern crisis intervention. According to Parad (1971, p. 196), Lindemann's classic study of bereaved disaster victims of the Coconut Grove nightclub fire in 1943 set the stage for the study and development of crisis theory and practice. Lindemann continued to refine his crisis concepts and in 1948 organized an innovative community mental health program in Boston called the Wellesley Human Relations Service. Through the auspices of this agency, Lindemann and his colleague, Gerald Caplan, continued to refine and explicate the use of short-term treatment and crisis intervention. Yet according to Rapoport (1970, p. 269), Lindemann and Caplan's ideas were slow in being adopted by other theorists. In her opinion, the prestige associated with the long-term psychotherapeutic model prevented many people from seriously considering crisis intervention as a treatment model.

At this point, is should be emphasized that much of the development of crisis intervention, particularly during the 1950's, went hand-in-hand with brief or short-term treatment. Rapoport (1970) describes this historical development. In fact, the very title of her article reflects this parallel development of crisis intervention and short-term treatment: "Crisis Intervention as a Mode of Brief Treatment". In this article, Rapoport (1970, pp. 270-271) states that

Bertha Reynolds' contributions from the functional school of casework along with Perlman's concept of "focus" in problem-solving helped greatly in reinforcing some of Lindemann and Caplan's concepts on crisis intervention. In addition, Perlman's (1963) article entitled "Some Notes on the Waiting List" further encouraged helping professions, especially social work, to look for other models of intervention besides extended psychotherapy. In many instances, Lindemann and Caplan's model of crisis intervention was seen as at least a partial remedy for desperately needed treatment plans. In summary, Rapoport (1970, p. 271) links the development of crisis intervention during the 1950's to four factors: (1) the need to serve more people, (2) the gap between needs and resources to meet those needs, (3) research that questioned the effectiveness of traditional methods, and (4) new systems of intervention such as crisis treatment.

If the 1950's marked the parallel development of crisis intervention and short-term treatment, the 1960's and the 1970's might be best characterized by the further refinement of crisis theory and practice and its separation from brief treatment as well as other intervention models. Building on the pioneering work of Lindemann and Caplan, other crisis theorists including Parad (1966, 1968, 1971), Rapoport (1962b, 1967, 1970), Jacobsen (1965a, 1968, 1970), and Aguilera (1967, 1970b) started not only to refine crisis theory but also to develop treatment models that could be used in marital and family conflicts, emergency hospitalization, suicide prevention, and other problems of living commonly referred to as crisis situations.

Purpose of the Study

Although many crisis theorists consider crisis intervention
to be a proven theory of social intervention, other critics (Bloom,
1963; Mackey, 1968; Pasewark, 1972) believe it is not yet a well
defined treatment model. For example, in Allen Darbonne's (1968)
research article entitled "Crisis: A Review of Theory, Practice, and
Research", he reported that crisis intervention as a conceptual framework and as a practice method is still unclear and cannot at this time
be regarded as a sound method of social intervention. In the writer's
own preliminary review of the literature on crisis intervention, he
also found this to be true. Therefore, the purposes of this study
were: (1) To review and compare the various conceptual frameworks
that have been used to describe crisis intervention; (2) To examine
and describe how these various conceptual frameworks of crisis intervention have been operationalized into practice with such selected
problems of living as marital and family conflicts, emergency hospitalization, suicide, etc.; (3) To analyze the similarities and differences
between these various conceptual frameworks and practices of crisis
intervention and planned short-term treatment; (4) To develop a general
conceptual framework for crisis intervention that can be operationalized
into practice across a variety of problem areas. In examining these
four objectives, the study consisted in large part of an exhaustive
research, review, and reconceptualization of the literature on crisis
intervention.

Organization of the Report

In organizing the report, the writer divided the study into four parts. The first part includes the purposes of the study along with the methodology designed to complete the research. The second part involves an examination of the theoretical contributions of those theorists whom most crisis authors consider to be the leading crisis intervention experts. In part three, the writer presents a review of the major practice areas of crisis intervention. The final part of the study first involves an analysis of the similarities and differences between crisis intervention and planned short-term treatment. Finally, the writer concludes the study with his own general theory of crisis intervention along with recommendations for the future growth and development of crisis intervention theory and practice.

CHAPTER II

METHODOLOGY

Research Design

Because this study consisted in large part of an exhaustive
research and review of the literature on crisis intervention, an
obvious question was how the literature could best be reviewed.
After careful consideration, it was decided that two major computer
search programs offered through the services of the University of Utah
library would be used along with a hand search of various publications.
A more exact accounting of these two major computer search programs
and the hand search of the literature will be presented in the section
of this study dealing with the identification and retrieval of data.

In assessing the data collected from the literature, various
publications were reviewed. In pre-assessing the literature, it was
first noted what publications dealt with the stated purposes and
objectives of the research. After this preliminary screening of the
literature was completed, those publications that dealt with the
stated purposes and objectives of the study were further analyzed in
terms of the assessment framework that was formulated to guide the
study. After the examination of the literature was completed, the
data were presented in terms of the stated purposes and objectives
of the research along with the following assessment framework.

Assessment Framework

Since the first purpose of this study was to review and compare
the various conceptual frameworks that have been used to describe
crisis intervention, there was an obvious need to formulate systematic
procedures that could be used in assessing the literature dealing with
crisis intervention theory. Hall and Lindzey (1970, pp. 19-27) struggled
with a similar problem when they tried to assess different theories
of personality. This was also the concern of Roberts and Nee (1970,
pp. 358-360) when they tried to assess eight different conceptual
frameworks and theories of social casework. In reviewing and comparing
the various conceptual frameworks that have been used to describe
crisis intervention, the assessment framework used in this study
incorporated the following criteria from the writings of Briar and
Miller (1971), Roberts and Nee (1970), and Vincent (1972):

1. How is the term "crisis" conceptualized?

   a. What constitutes a crisis? Is the definition clear and precise
      or clouded?

   b. Are there different stages of a crisis? Are these stages clear
      and precise? Do they correspond with the overall definition
      of a crisis?

   c. Is there any attempt to classify different types of crisis?
      Are these classifications specific or generalized?

2. How is the practice of crisis intervention conceptualized?

   a. Is there a designated study phase? What characterizes the
      study process?

   b. How is the diagnosis or assessment stage of treatment concept-
      ualized?

      (1)   How is the client assessed? Are differential diagnoses or assessments made? What classification scheme is used?

      (2)   How are the treatment strategies designed? Are the treatment strategies classified and described?

  c. How are the treatment strategies implemented?

      (1)   Are the treatment strategies clear and precise?

      (2)   Do the treatment strategies relate to specific crisis problems or are they general treatment strategies?

      (3)   Is there any attempt to define the client-worker-agency relationship in these treatment strategies?

      (4)   Are the treatment strategies inclusive within the client-worker-agency structure or are other community resources used?

      (5)   How is the treatment outcome assessed? Are these assessment criteria specific or generalized?

3. How is the conceptual framework of crisis intervention related to other conceptual frameworks and theories of human behavior and social intervention, i.e. ego psychology, existentialism, etc?

  a. What other conceptual frameworks or theories of human behavior and social intervention are referred to?

  b. In using these other conceptual frameworks and theories, have they added to their meaning, i.e. definitions, concepts, treatment strategies, etc., or merely drawn from them?

4. What empirical validation, if any, is there for the particular conceptual framework of crisis intervention?

  a. Has the conceptual framework been empirically tested before?

  b. What method of empirical research was used, i.e. pre-research or observation, exploratory and formulative, descriptive, experimental?

  c. What sampling method was used? To what advantage or disadvantage?

  d. How were the data collected? Were the measurements taken reliable and valid?

  e. How were the data analyzed and interpreted? Were the results significant? Can the results be understood, communicated, and applied?

5. What appear to be the difficulties of relating the generalizations of the conceptual framework to the practice of crisis intervention?

    a. Is it useful as a major focus for assessment or treatment, or both?

    b. Are there any unsolved problems or questions?

The second purpose of this study was to examine and describe from the literature how these various conceptual frameworks of crisis intervention have been operationalized into practice and used with selected problems of living. In selecting what problems of living would be examined, a brief review of the literature revealed that crisis intervention was most often used with: (1) childhood and adolescent crises, (2) mental health problems, (3) marital and family conflicts, (4) emergency hospitalization, and (5) suicide prevention. This list was not, of course, a complete description of the various problems of living that can be affected by crisis intervention. Rather, the list was proposed as a tentative description of various crisis intervention practice areas. In examining these and other areas of crisis intervention practice, the study assessed practice in terms of the following model that has been used by various authors (Briar and Miller, 1971; Reid and Shyne, 1969; Roberts and Nee, 1970; Vincent, 1972):

1. How were direct services given to the client(s)?

    a. How did the client reach the worker and/or the agency?

    b. Who determined that the client's problem constituted a crisis?

2. What did these direct services consist of?

    a. What happened during the initial or study phase of treatment? What characterized the study process?

b. How was the client's problem assessed? What classification system, if any, was used?

c. What treatment strategies were used? How were the treatment strategies classified, i.e. supportive, reflective, confrontive, etc?

d. Who implemented the treatment strategies?

e. What was the basis of the client-worker-agency relationship?

f. How was the length and intensity of treatment required assessed? What criteria were used in determining if the client was ready for termination?

3. How were these direct services evaluated?

a. What method of empirical research was used, i.e. pre-research or observation, exploratory and formulative, descriptive, and experimental?

b. What sampling method was used? To what advantage or disadvantage?

c. How were the data collected? Were the measurements taken reliable and valid?

d. How were the data analyzed and interpreted? Were the results significant? Can the results be understood, communicated, and applied?

4. How closely did these direct services reflect the conceptual framework of crisis intervention that they were using?

a. Did the initial or study, assessment or diagnosis, and treatment stages relate back to the conceptual framework?

b. Were the client-worker-agency practice relationships compatible with the conceptual framework?

c. What appeared to be the major difficulty, if any, in relating the generalizations of the conceptual framework to the actual process of crisis intervention?

d. Were there any unsolved problems or questions?

The third purpose of this study was to analyze the similarities and differences between these various conceptual frameworks and practices

of crisis intervention and planned short-term treatment. According
to Reid and Shyne (1969), "planned short-term service is conducted
under the assumptions that the contact will be limited...planned
short-term treatment by its design forces limitations on the problems
to be dealt with and the scope of the objectives [pp. 3-4]". Many
experts (Parad, 1968; Rapoport, 1967; Reid and Epstein, 1972; Reid
and Shyne, 1969) recognize that there are similarities between crisis
intervention and planned short-term treatment. Most of these same
experts also agree that there are striking differences between the
two modalities of social intervention. Although a considerable amount
has been written on planned short-term treatment, two studies continue
to stand out from the rest: Reid and Shyne's (1969) Brief and Extended
Casework and Reid and Epstein's (1972) Task-Centered Casework. These
two studies were used in comparing and contrasting crisis intervention
with planned short-term treatment. In comparing and contrasting these
two methods of social intervention, the following criteria were used
which were again incorporated from other sources (Briar and Miller,
1971; Roberts and Nee, 1970) and added to:

1. What are the similarities and differences in the problems of
   living crisis intervention and planned short-term treatment deal
   with?

   a. What specific problems of living are both successful in
      treating?

   b. Are there certain problems of living that one method of social
      intervention is more successful with than the other?

   c. What problems of living are neither method of social inter-
      vention suitable in treating?

2. Are there similarities and differences in the stages and assessment of treatment?

    a. How do both methods of social intervention deal with the initial or study phase of treatment?

    b. What are the similarities and differences in their descriptions of the assessment or diagnosis stage?

    c. Are there similarities and differences in treatment strategies?

    d. How do they assess the length and intensity of treatment required?

    e. What methods and procedures do they use in assessing treatment outcome?

3. What are the similarities and differences in the assessment of the client-worker-agency relationship?

    a. How do they view the client?

    b. What responsibility do they place with the client for his own treatment?

    c. Are there similarities and differences in the client-worker-agency roles?

4. What concepts and practice principles have the two methods of social intervention drawn from other conceptual frameworks and theories of human behavior and social intervention, i.e. ego psychology, existentialism, etc?

    a. What conceptual frameworks and theories of human behavior and social intervention have the concepts and practice principles been drawn?

    b. In drawing from these concepts and practice principles, i.e. client-worker-agency relationship, treatment strategies, etc., have they added to their meaning or merely restated the concept or practice principle?

The final purpose of the study was to develop a general conceptual framework for crisis intervention that could be operationalized into practice across a variety of problem areas. In developing and assessing this general framework for crisis intervention, the model partly developed by Briar and Miller (1971), Roberts and Nee (1970), and Vincent (1972) was again used (see pages 8-10).

Identification and Retrieval of Data

In identifying and retrieving the literature on crisis intervention, two major computer search programs offered through the University of Utah library were used. ERIC (The Educational Research Information Center) is a nationwide information center designed and operated by the U. S. Department of Education. Through a network of 18 decentralized clearinghouses ERIC acquires, abstracts, indexes, stores, retrieves, and disseminates the most significant and up-to-date documents on many aspects of professional education including counseling services and programs. In using the ERIC system, a copy of the stated purposes and objectives of the study was sent to the clearinghouse center in Michigan that dealt with counseling services. There the professional literature dealing with crisis intervention was reviewed. When the literature search was completed, the ERIC clearinghouse sent back a computerized listing of all pertinent literature in their files that dealt with crisis intervention and the stated purposes and objectives of the study. Accompanying that computerized listing was a short abstract of each publication describing briefly its contents. From that computerized listing, each article and publication that dealt with the stated purposes and objectives of the study were further analyzed.

A second computer search program used was DATRIX. DATRIX is a data collection agency sponsored by the Xerox Corporation that searches and reviews dissertation abstracts around a specific research question.

In using DATRIX, key words and phrases were identified to guide the computer search. In the case of this study, such key words and phrases as "crisis", "stress", "therapy", "crisis intervention", "crisis treatment", "critical areas", "emergency psychiatric care", etc., were forwarded to the DATRIX center along with the stated purposes and objectives of the study. The DATRIX center, in turn, researched and reviewed dissertation abstracts around these key words, phrases, and purposes and objectives of the study and then forwarded a computerized listing of those dissertations that dealt with the study. These dissertations were then further researched through the University of Utah library services.

In addition to these two major computer search programs, the study also included a hand search of various publications and articles dealing with crisis intervention up to and including those for December of 1972. This hand search of the literature included the following general reference indexes:

1. Dissertation Abstracts

2. International Index to Periodicals

3. Public Affairs Information Service

4. Psychological Abstracts

5. Readers' Guide to Periodical Literature

6. Social Work Abstracts

7. Sociological Abstracts

In searching through these general reference indexes, every attempt was made to locate information dealing with crisis intervention and the stated purposes and objectives of the study. In order to do this, a systematic procedure was followed. For example, the indexes of each of these general references were reviewed in terms of the following subtopics that dealt with different aspects of crisis intervention: crisis, stress, therapy, treatment, crisis intervention, critical areas, emergency psychiatric care, and other appropriate crisis intervention subtopics. Selected bibliographies dealing with crisis intervention were also used to research and review the literature. These selected bibliographies were solicited from interested faculty members as well as from a number of staff personnel working in crisis intervention centers and agencies throughout the Salt Lake City area.

Finally, after each publication and article was reviewed, the bibliographies accompanying those articles were reviewed to identify additional literature dealing with crisis intervention. This final check was included to help ensure a maximum coverage of pertinent crisis intervention publications and articles.

Data Analysis and Presentation

In analyzing the literature, two basic steps were followed. First each publication and article was analyzed in terms of the assessment framework that accompanied the first objective of the study (see Assessment Framework in Chapter Two, pages 8-14). When that was completed, each publication and article that dealt with the practice of crisis intervention was also analyzed in terms of the assessment framework that accompanied the second objective of the study. Then the data collected from these two assessment frameworks were used in completing the final two objectives of the study.

After all the appropriate data had been identified, retrieved, and analyzed, the results were presented in terms of the assessment framework that accompanied each of the four objectives of the study. This assessment framework was used to present the data in an orderly and systematic manner.

PART II

THEORIES OF CRISIS INTERVENTION

CHAPTER III

ERICH LINDEMANN AND GERALD CAPLAN

Introduction

In order to present the more important conceptual frameworks of
crisis intervention, it became necessary to select those authors who
had contributed most to the growth and development of crisis intervention theory and practice. After researching the literature, the writer
found that most authors regard the following theorists as the leading
crisis intervention experts: Erich Lindemann and Gerald Caplan,
Lydia Rapoport, Howard J. Parad, Gerald F. Jacobsen, and Donna C.
Aguilera. Consequently, it was decided to review and evaluate in depth
the crisis intervention theories of these recognized experts. Although
primary consideration was given to researching the theories of these
crisis experts, the contributions of other crisis authors were also
reviewed.

Since most experts (Aguilera, 1970b; Parad, 1970; Rapoport, 1970)
regard Erich Lindemann as the father of crisis intervention, it is only
natural to begin any analysis of crisis theory by first examining his
pioneering work. In analyzing Lindemann's work, it soon became
apparent, however, that one could not consider his work without also
discussing the contributions of his colleague, Gerald Caplan. Together
they formulated the first conceptual framework of crisis intervention

theory and practice. This contribution is acknowledged by most crisis
theorists who usually discuss Lindemann and Caplan's theories of crisis
intervention as if they were one work. Therefore, the following
discussion includes the crisis intervention theories of both Lindemann
and Caplan.

Crisis Conceptualization

In examining Lindemann's (1944) first article on crisis intervention, the writer quickly noted the absence of terms like "crisis"
or "crisis intervention". Instead, Lindemann directed most of his
discussion to the analysis of "acute grief" experienced by the disaster
victims of the Coconut Grove nightclub fire in 1943. Yet, in describing
the characteristics of acute grief, Lindemann established the basic
framework for defining the symptomatology of a crisis reaction. In
observing the nature of the grief reaction, Lindemann (1944, pp. 141-
142) was impressed by three striking features:

1. The marked tendency to sighing respiration; this respiration
   disturbance was most conspicuous when the patient was made
   to discuss his grief.

2. The complaint about lack of strength and exhaustion which
   is universal and is described as follows: "It is almost
   impossible to climb up a stairway".

3. Digestive symptoms, described as follows: "The food tastes
   like sand", etc.

In addition, Lindemann believed most people experiencing grief reactions
struggled with feelings of increased emotional distance from other people.

Based on these observations, Lindemann concluded that most people
experiencing acute grief usually have five related reactions: (1) somatic

distress, (2) preoccupation with the image of the deceased, (3) guilt, (4) hostile reactions, and (5) loss of patterns of conduct. In addition, Lindemann also found that the stages and duration of a grief reaction seem to depend upon the success with which a person does his "grief work". Generally, this grief work includes achieving emancipation from the deceased, readjustment to the environment in which the deceased is missing, and the formation of new relationships.

Through his research, Lindemann (1944, p. 143) also found that in some instances there is a delayed grief reaction, particularly when the affected person has been confronted with essential tasks and has had to assist in maintaining the morale of others. Yet, when this period has passed, the person almost always finds himself experiencing grief. For those who do not experience a delayed grief reaction, the immediate impact of bereavement can bring a number of distorted reactions that include: (1) overactivity without a sense of loss, (2) the acquisition of symptoms belonging to the last illness of the deceased, (3) a recognized medical disease (ulcerative colitis, asthma, etc.), and (4) agitated depression.

To this point in the discussion, it has been shown that part of Lindemann's early contributions to crisis intervention centers on the symptomatology of a crisis. The detailed description of a crisis reaction was refined to such a degree by Gerald Caplan that Morley (1970, p. 15) has referred to him as the "Father of Modern Crisis Intervention". It was Caplan, in fact, who first associated the concept of homeostasis with crisis intervention. According to Caplan (1964, pp. 39-40), the human organism constantly endeavors to maintain a homeo-

static balance with the outside environment. When this delicate
balance is threatened by either physiological or psychological forces,
the human organism engages in problem-solving activities designed to
restore this delicate balance. In a crisis situation, however, the
individual is faced with a problem that appears to have no immediate
solution, hence the idea that a crisis is an upset of a steady or
homeostatic state. Caplan (1964) explained this point further by
saying that "the problem is one where the individual is faced by
stimuli which signal danger to a fundamental need satisfaction or
evoke major need appetite, and the circumstances are such that habitual problem-solving methods are unsuccessful within the time span of
past expectations of success [p. 39]". In summary, Caplan defined a
crisis as an upset of a steady state where the individual is faced
with an obstacle, usually to important life goals, that cannot be
overcome through ordinary methods of problem-solving.

Along with introducing the concept of homeostasis, Caplan also
attempted to define and describe the different stages of a crisis.
According to Caplan (1964, pp. 40-41; 1965, pp. 150-151), a crisis
is a time-limited period of disequilibrium or homeostatic imbalance
that generally follows four stages. The first stage of crisis is the
initial rise in tension that results from the crisis provoking event.
When this tension begins to mount, the individual will usually try to
resolve the crisis by using familiar patterns of problem-solving
behavior. The second stage of crisis is characterized by increased
tension because the individual has not yet resolved the crisis.
During this second stage, emergency problem-solving skills are often

used to reduce the tension. As these emergency activities fail to alleviate the tension, the individual enters the third stage of crisis. Now the tension becomes so great that the individual may experience acute depression because he feels so helpless and lost. As he enters the final stage of crisis, one of two things usually happens. If the tension continues to increase, he may experience a major emotional and mental breakdown. On the other hand, he may resolve the crisis by using maladaptive patterns of behavior that decrease tension but impair his future social functioning.

Although Lindemann presented only a brief description of the different types of crises, Caplan discussed them in some depth. In so doing, he used Erikson's (1950, 1956) model of developmental and accidental crises. Caplan has defined developmental crises as transitional periods in personality development characterized by cognitive and affective upset. Common examples of these types of crises are birth, infancy, childhood, adolescence, adulthood, and old-age. On the other hand, accidental crises are described as periods of psychological and behavioral upset that are precipitated by life hazards involving significant losses such as illness and death. In addition, Caplan emphasizes that developmental and accidental crises are transitional periods that present the individual with both an opportunity for personal growth as well as emotional and mental deterioration. This concept will be discussed more carefully in the section that follows on treatment strategies.

Treatment Conceptualization

Lindemann has presented a sketchy conceptualization of crisis intervention practice. Still, it is possible to reconstruct part of his treatment plan under the following general headings: initial or study phase, assessment or diagnosis, and treatment strategies. To begin with, Lindemann (1944, p. 147) emphasized that proper psychiatric management of crisis reactions may prevent prolonged and serious alterations in the patient's social adjustment. Although he did not identify it as the thrust of the initial phase of treatment, Lindemann (1944) did state that "the essential task facing the psychiatrist is that of sharing the patient's grief work, that is, his efforts at extricating himself from the bondage to the deceased and at finding new patterns of rewarding interaction [p. 147]". This introduces one of the fundamental aspects of crisis intervention practice — immediate access to the client.

Caplan (1964) has not shed much additional light on the initial or study phase of crisis practice, although he has reinforced Lindemann's concept of immediate access to the client. In addition, Caplan (1964) stressed that the client's family must be involved as soon as possible in helping with the crisis:

> The important point for maintenance of mental health and avoidance of mental disorder is that the activities of the family or other primary groups be directed to helping the person in crisis deal with his problem by some form of activity rather than avoid the problem or restrict his activity to tension [p. 45].

Lindemann and Caplan have said even less about the assessment or diagnosis stage of treatment. For example, Lindemann's (1944) only comment was "that patients with obsessive personality make-up and with a history of former depressions are likely to develop an agitated depression [p. 146]". Actually, this statement does not tell much about how the client's crisis should be assessed so the most effective treatment strategies can be used. In a later article, however, Lindemann and Klein (1961) implied that the assessment of a crisis situation needs to include the client's interactions with the outer world. In addition, both authors maintained that the assessment stage should be concerned with determining whether or not a crisis really exists, although no crisis criteria were offered to guide this assessment. Caplan (1964) somewhat clouded the issue further by stating that "because this aspect of their work [referring to assessment] has seldom been made explicit, there is no defined approach to it in most of these care-giving professions, so the behavior of professionals in this area cannot be differentiated along the lines of professional boundaries... [p. 51]".

With respect to the implementation of treatment strategies, both Lindemann and Caplan have presented a clearer picture of crisis practice. Lindemann began by saying that the essential task facing the therapist is that of sharing the client's grief work. Stated another way, crisis intervention is best implemented when the therapist shares the impact of the crisis with the client. Lindemann (1944, p. 147) clarified this point further by emphasizing that during the crisis of bereavement the therapist needs to help the client accomplish the following tasks or goals:

1. Accept the pain of bereavement.

2. Review his relationship with the deceased and become acquainted with the alterations in his own modes of emotional reaction.

3. Express sorrow and sense of loss.

4. Find an acceptable formulation of his future relationships to the deceased.

5. Verbalize his feelings of guilt and find persons around him whom he can use as "primers" for the acquisition of new patterns of conduct.

In his discussion of crisis intervention strategies, Caplan (1960, 1964, 1965) has stressed that crisis reactions are time-limited, usually lasting six to eight weeks. In addition, the type of treatment given to a client during this crisis period may not only reestablish his pre-crisis level of functioning but also improve it. In the writer's opinion, Caplan has not clearly described what this crisis treatment must consist of to be effective. If he has stressed the implementation of any treatment strategy, it has been the client's need to accomplish certain tasks or goals. In so doing, Caplan has mirrored the earlier ideas of Lindemann and his treatment goals for bereavement. As the conceptual framework of crisis intervention has continued to develop, later theorists have referred to these treatment goals as psychological tasks that the therapist needs to help the client accomplish. This use of psychological tasks in crisis treatment has been described particularly well by Rapoport (1962b) and Kaplan (1965) in their studies of crisis intervention with families of premature children.

Both Lindemann and Caplan discuss the use of other resources in helping a client resolve his crisis successfully. How these other resources are used is not clearly defined, although Lindemann acknowledges the inherent advantages of certain religious organizations in dealing with the crisis of bereavement. Caplan (1964, p. 48) reinforces this idea by stating that the people who most strongly affect an individual during a crisis are those who are linked to him through his basic needs for love and interaction. This is one reason why Caplan encourages the involvement of the family in crisis treatment.

In Lindemann's (1944) first article on bereavement, there is no mention of how crisis treatment should be effectively terminated or evaluated. In a later article, Lindemann and Klein (1961, p. 292) state that termination should be considered when the proposed limited goals of treatment have been optimally attained and a feeling of continued confidence exists toward the worker and agency. Put another way, Lindemann is saying that termination should be seriously considered only when the client has accomplished the psychological tasks associated with the successful resolution of the crisis. At that time, the therapist reviews with the client what he has accomplished in working through the crisis. Still, Lindemann has little to say about how treatment should be evaluated other than the therapist's personal evaluation of whether or not the client resolved the crisis effectively.

Caplan (1960, 1964, 1965) offers little additional insight into the termination of crisis services and their evaluation. In his book Principles of Preventive Psychiatry (1964), he does include the following statement about the possible outcomes of crisis practice:

> The outcome will be determined by choices
> which are made partly actively and partly by chance
> and by other aspects of the situation. The bodily

> state of the individual at the time, the pure chance
> aspects of the development of the external stress,
> the availability of external social resources, and
> the communication system of the milieu are all
> important, as well as the personality of the individ-
> ual, which is the psychological crystallization of
> his experience [p. 41].

In the writer's estimation, this statement tells very little about treatment outcome or evaluation. Unfortunately, it is one of the few statements Caplan has ever written on treatment outcome.

Relationship to other Theories

In Lindemann's (1944, 1956, 1961) various articles and publications on grief reactions and crisis theory, the writer found few, if
any, discussions of how his crisis concepts were related to other
theories. Since Lindemann's professional training in psychiatry
stressed the use of the psychoanalytic model, it is likely that this
previous training influenced some of his ideas. In her book on crisis
intervention, Aguilera (1970b, p. 4) argues convincingly that Lindemann
was particularly influenced by Erikson's theories of ego psychology,
especially his concepts of developmental and accidental crises and the
eight stages of human development. According to Aguilera, Lindemann's
interest in Erikson's developmental theory lead him to an examination
of approaches that could prevent emotional and mental disorganization
during these developmental and accidental crises. The result of
Lindemann's work was the birth of crisis theory.

Caplan, like Lindemann, refers to Erikson's theories of ego
psychology but does not claim they are the basis of his theory.
Instead, Aguilera (1970b, p. 5) believes that Caplan's concepts of

homeostasis and organismic equilibrium are adapted from Sandor Rado's
adaptational psychodynamics theory. Nevertheless, in drawing some of
these concepts from other theorists, Lindemann and Caplan added much
to their meaning. The writer feels this is particularly true of their
work on the stages and treatment of a crisis reaction.

Empirical Validation

The great bulk of Lindemann's (1944) research was done by
observing the reactions of 101 clients experiencing grief reactions
after the Coconut Grove nightclub fire in 1943. His research consists
of a series of psychiatric interviews that were used in recording and
analyzing the crisis reactions of these patients. Consequently, almost
all of Lindemann's research reports the findings of these psychological
observations. In many ways, this may account for Lindemann's sketchy
coverage of crisis practice. Yet, in the writer's opinion, the practice
concepts of crisis treatment should have had a higher priority with
Lindemann. By limiting his research to the symptomatology of grief
reactions, he did a great service in crystallizing some of the more
important concepts of crisis theory. Yet, his limited conceptualization
of crisis practice reduced the immediate impact of crisis intervention
as a treatment model.

Like Lindemann, Caplan's (1960) earlier research on crisis
intervention describes different crisis responses. For example, in
his article published in 1960 he reports on the patterns of parental
response to the crisis of premature birth. In this study, however,
Caplan does not mention how many patients successfully resolved the

crisis. Instead, he only describes their crisis reactions. In 1965, Caplan wrote an article entitled "Four Studies of Crisis in Parents of Prematures" where he evaluated crisis treatment in terms of the client's successful completion of certain psychological tasks. In this outcome study, Caplan found that those mothers who consistently visited their premature babies more often overcame the crisis of prematurity than those mothers who were inconsistent in their visiting patterns. This finding, in the writer's judgment, is one reason why more recent crisis theorists (Parad, 1968, 1971; Rapoport, 1967, 1970; Aguilera, 1970b) are still emphasizing the use of psychological tasks and problem-solving activities in crisis treatment.

Unresolved Issues and Problems

The pioneering work of Lindemann and Caplan did a number of things to influence the further development of crisis theory and practice. To begin with, both men concentrated much of their efforts on the observation of crisis symptomatology. This, among other things, showed conclusively that crises were time-limited and could be opportunities for growth as well as for emotional upheaval, depending on the nature and quality of treatment received by the client. Their detailed observations of the crisis stages helped later theorists and practitioners in understanding what to expect from a person embroiled in a crisis. In addition, Lindemann and Caplan's use of specific psychological tasks or goals in bringing crises like bereavement and prematurity to a successful resolution encouraged other theorists to investigate the use of tasks in crisis treatment.

As theorists, however, Lindemann and Caplan were less thorough in explicating crisis intervention practice. This is understandable because a theoretical framework usually precedes a practice framework. Before Lindemann and Caplan could successfully treat crisis reactions, they first needed to know more about what constituted a crisis. This they did very well.

Conclusion

All crisis theorists acknowledge the pioneering work of Lindemann and Caplan. They were the first researchers to systematically observe and describe the characteristics of the crisis reaction. Other theorists added to this conceptualization of crisis intervention with varying degrees of success. The initial thrust, however, was made by these two acknowledged leaders of crisis intervention.

CHAPTER IV

LYDIA RAPOPORT

Introduction

Much of Lydia Rapoport's conceptual framework of crisis theory
and practice is a further refinement of the basic crisis concepts of
Lindemann and Caplan with some important additions. One of these
additions concerns the further development of crisis practice and its
linkage with other models of social intervention. In fact, Lydia
Rapoport was one of the first crisis theorists to discuss this obvious
linkage of crisis intervention with other treatment models.

Crisis Conceptualization

In her first article entitled "The State of Crisis: Some
Theoretical Considerations", Rapoport (1962a) defined a crisis as
"an upset of a steady state" where an individual finds himself in a
hazardous situation. This brief definition was first formulated by
Lindemann and Caplan. After rephrasing some of Caplan's (1964) ideas
on homeostasis, Rapoport mentioned that in a state of crisis the normal
problem-solving mechanisms of the individual are not adequate to
achieve a balanced state which throws the individual into disequilibrium.
In her later articles (1967, 1970), Rapoport continued to use these
same crisis concepts that were borrowed from Lindemann and Caplan.

In reviewing Rapoport's (1962a, 1967, 1970) publications on
crisis, it is obvious that she did help refine some of Lindemann and
Caplan's major crisis concepts. For example, Rapoport's (1962a, pp.
212-214) first publication emphasized that a crisis situation creates
a problem that can be perceived as a threat, a loss, or a challenge.
Then she added that three interrelated factors usually produce a state
of crisis: (1) a hazardous event, (2) a threat to life goals, and
(3) an inability to respond with adequate coping mechanisms. In their
earlier writings, Lindemann (1944) and Caplan (1964) talked somewhat
about the hazardous event that produces a crisis. Rapoport, however,
describes more clearly the nature of this crisis producing event.
This, in the writer's judgment, is an important contribution because
with the increasing development of crisis theory and practice emphasis
has been placed on identifying the precipitating factor that lead to
the crisis. In fact, in Bloom's (1963) study on the "Definitional
Aspects of the Crisis Concepts" he reports that crisis therapists
could only agree that a stressful situation is a crisis when a known
precipitating event can be identified.

Whereas Caplan (1964) discussed four phases of a crisis reaction,
Rapoport (1962a, 1967, 1970) identified three phases: (1) initial or
beginning, (2) middle, and (3) end. During the initial or beginning
phase of crisis, there is a rise in tension due to the stressful
precipitating event. This tension forces the individual to apply
habitual problem-solving mechanisms to the crisis situation. If these
traditional problem-solving mechanisms fail, tension increases and the
individual moves into the middle phase of crisis. Now emergency

problem-solving mechanisms such as denial, flight into health, etc., are applied to the crisis. These emergency mechanisms result in one of three conclusions: (1) problem solved, (2) problem redefined, or (3) problem denied. All crisis reactions have an end phase when some type of equilibrium is restored. Yet this equilibrium can be the same, lower, or higher than the one that occurred previous to the crisis. Here, Rapoport reflected Lindemann's (1944) earlier notion that a crisis can be a growth producing experience if the client receives the right type of help.

In discussing these various phases or stages of a crisis, Rapoport (1962a, 1967, 1970) also emphasized that a crisis is time-limited, usually lasting six to eight weeks. In addition, she emphasized Lindemann and Caplan's notion that during such a crisis the individual is particularly amenable to help if the right type of help is given. Once again, the concept of immediate access to the crisis client was reinforced.

In Rapoport's 1962a article she did mention different types of crises. However, in her (1967, 1970) later articles she classified crises into three different categories: (1) developmental crises which are bio-psycho-social in nature, (2) crises of role transition, and (3) accidental crises, termed hazardous events. Basically, these are the same types of crises that Caplan (1964) discussed in an earlier article which he borrowed from the writings of Erikson (1950, 1956).

Treatment Conceptualization

In Rapoport's (1962a) earlier article on crisis intervention,

she presented an abbreviated conceptualization of crisis practice.
However, in her (1967, 1970) later articles she developed a much
clearer treatment model. In discussing the initial or study phase
of treatment, Rapoport began by saying that in order to help people
who are in a state of crisis the worker needs to have rapid access
to them and they need to have rapid access to the worker. She (1967)
reinforced this idea with the following statement: "A little help,
rationally directed and purposively focused at a strategic time, is
more effective than more extensive help given at a period of less
emotional assessibility [p. 38]".

In a later article, Rapoport (1970, pp. 286-292) made the
initial or study phase of crisis practice even clearer. She began
by saying that it is almost impossible to describe the initial phase
in crisis treatment without referring to the entire treatment process.
Still, she feels that during the initial interview the primary task
of the worker is to develop a tentative diagnosis of the presenting
problem. Even more important, during the initial interview the worker
should convey a sense of hope and enthusiasm to the client concerning
the successful resolution of the crisis. In order to do this, Rapoport
believes that the initial contact with the client should include a
mutual exploration of the problem along with clearly defined goals or
tasks that will successfully resolve the crisis. This conveys hope to
the client that the crisis can be resolved and that he and the therapist
will be working together.

In describing the assessment stage of treatment, Rapoport
mentions that it is combined with the initial or study phase because of

the need for immediate help. Therefore, in assessing the crisis problem primary emphasis is placed on identifying with the client what event or situation precipitated the crisis and why the client has not been able to resolve the problem successfully. Rapoport does not explain how the client is actively involved in this assessment, though the later works of Jacobsen (1970) and Aguilera (1970b) further clarify the client's involvement in the assessment stage. In addition, one of the most important characteristics of the assessment stage is a consideration of what psychological tasks or goals will help resolve the crisis.

In arriving at treatment strategies, Rapoport stresses the need to identify specific problem-solving tasks to achieve a healthy resolution of the crisis. This, of course, was first introduced by Lindemann (1944) when he outlined the tasks that were necessary to resolve successfully the crisis of bereavement. Rapoport (1962b, p. 50) used this concept when she worked with mothers experiencing the crisis of a premature birth. According to her article, she feels a mother hospitalized along with a premature infant needs to accomplish a series of psychological tasks which include an acknowledgment that the infant's life is threatened and that survival in the early postnatal period may be uncertain. Then, as the child's situation improves, Rapoport designs additional psychological tasks that then need to be accomplished. For instance, when the premature child is finally able to join the mother at home the task becomes helping the mother assume the nurturing role, along with providing attention sensitively to the special needs of the child.

In implementing her treatment strategies, Rapoport presents
a clear and precise treatment strategy, but only as it relates to the
crisis of a premature birth. Still, her use of psychological tasks
can be applied to other crisis situations as long as the appropriate
psychological tasks can be identified. In fact, Rapoport (1970,
pp. 296-297) stresses this very point in her latest article on crisis
intervention. She even goes so far as to say that the minimum goals
of crisis-oriented treatment should include: (1) relief of symptoms,
(2) restoration to the optimal level of functioning that existed before
the present crisis, (3) understanding of the relevant precipitating
events that contributed to the state of disequilibrium, and (4) identification of remedial measures that can be taken by the client or family
that are available through community resources.

With this crisis approach, Rapoport (1970) believes the role
of the worker in the client-worker-agency relationship should be an
active and directive stance "not over time through elements of attach-
ment and transference, but on elements of authority based on expertness
and competence [p. 300]". It appears Rapoport is trying to stress that
since crisis treatment is time-limited, usually lasting six to eight
weeks, the therapist must be expert in identifying the psychological
tasks that the client needs to accomplish and then competent in aiding
the client in completing those tasks. With these psychological tasks
as a guide, Rapoport feels that any evaluation of crisis treatment must
be based on the successful accomplishment of these tasks.

By this time, it may have become apparent to the reader that
Rapoport has used many traditional treatment concepts as an important part

of her model. This is particularly true of her emphasis on identifying the problem, involving the client in his own treatment, and serving as a role model for the client. In fact, Rapoport (1970) acknowledged this relationship by saying:

> In sum then, from a technical point of view, crisis brief treatment makes use of all the principles and techniques which have been developed in casework methodology that are relevant and useful. However, there is a rendering of, and greater emphasis on, some techniques. The approach is more active, directive, and authoritarian. Time limits are used for a framework, to push toward problem-solving and to avoid regression. The client's capacity for autonomous action and decision is maximized. Treatment is highly focused and segmental, and problems to be worked are partialized [p. 301].

Relationship to other Theories

In Rapoport's (1962a, 1962b, 1967) earlier articles on crisis intervention she does not discuss the relationship of crisis theory and practice to other theories of human behavior and social intervention. Yet in her 1970 publication, Rapoport states that "crisis theory represents a synthesis of concepts, empirical observations, and clinical insights drawn from many behavioral and social science areas [p. 271]". Then she states that crisis theory is securely anchored in personality theory. Specifically, she refers to Erikson's developmental theory of personality growth and maturation. As noted earlier in this study, Lindemann (1944) and Caplan (1964) both acknowledged the contributions of Erikson to their respective theoretical frameworks.

In discussing crisis intervention and its relationship to other theories of human behavior, Rapoport also referred to the work of ego psychologists such as Hartman (1958), who were instrumental in describing how the human organism copes with a changing environment by continually striving to maintain a dynamic homeostasis or equilibrium. Then again, there are the earlier contributions of Freud and his daughter Anna who both discussed in detail how people cope with reality through an intricate system of defense mechanisms.

In summary, Rapoport has pointed out that crisis theory has obvious links with a variety of conceptual frameworks that include psychoanalysis, ego psychology, learning theory, and traditional social casework. In addition, Rapoport believes that crisis theory borrows heavily from the public health model of practice partially initiated by Lindemann and his associates at the Wellesley Human Relations Service.

Empirical Validation

In only one of Rapoport's (1962b) publications does she discuss in detail the empirical evaluation of crisis intervention and this evaluation is very sketchy. This particular article entitled "Working with Families in Crisis: An Exploration in Preventive Intervention" is a descriptive study of families struggling with the crisis of a premature birth. In the study, a total of 60 interviews were held with 11 families. The exact sampling methods are unclear and no detailed explanation of data collection or analysis is presented other than the subjective observations of the interviewers. The findings of the research project emphasize that those families who accomplish certain psychological tasks during the various stages of the crisis of premature birth have the best treatment outcomes. Yet, Rapoport does not mention what outcome criteria she was using other than the subjective evaluations of the interviewers.

The other publications of Rapoport (1962a, 1967, 1970) do not mention any empirical research conducted to assess the effectiveness of crisis treatment. Still, in most of these articles, Rapoport implies that any evaluation of crisis treatment needs to be centered on how successfully the client completes the crisis tasks. Rapoport (1967) reemphasizes this concept by saying that "termination takes place when a previously defined goal has been reached or when a client begins to find solutions [p. 40]".

Unresolved Issues and Problems

In the writer's opinion, Rapoport has presented a more comprehensive conceptualization of crisis practice than have Lindemann and Caplan. She discusses in some depth the importance of the initial and assessment stages of crisis intervention and then presents a thoughtful discussion of treatment implementation. It would appear one of her greatest contributions to crisis theory is the emphasis she places on the identification and successful completion of psychological tasks or goals. In fact, most of her discussion of crisis treatment focuses on the worker's efforts in helping the client accomplish these crisis tasks.

Like Lindemann and Caplan, however, Rapoport does not struggle with the all important question of treatment evaluation. What research she has done in the crisis area is limited to an identification of psychological tasks the accomplishment of which would help resolve the crisis of prematurity. Still, the only criteria she adopts in assessing whether these tasks were completed successfully are the subjective evaluations of the researchers. Later in the study, it will be shown that some practitioners are now using and devising specific psychological tests in an attempt to empirically evaluate the effectiveness of crisis intervention.

Conclusion

Rapoport has built much of her conceptualization of crisis theory and practice on the earlier research of Lindemann and Caplan. In building on that earlier conceptual model, Rapoport was one of the first crisis theorists to describe systematically the process of crisis treatment. This she accomplished well and, in so doing, further refined crisis theory and practice.

CHAPTER V

HOWARD J. PARAD

Introduction

Howard J. Parad has been for many years a close associate of
both Lindemann and Caplan. In fact, he was a colleague of both men
at the Wellesley Human Relations Service during the 1950's and 1960's.
Consequently, Parad's conceptualization of crisis theory and practice
has been greatly influenced by these two earlier pioneers of crisis
intervention. As with Rapoport, Parad's work constitutes a further
refinement of crisis theory along with a beginning conceptualization
of crisis practice. Still, it appears to the writer that Parad does
not reflect in his articles and publications the same clarity of theory
and practice as Rapoport. However, let the reader judge for himself.

Crisis Conceptualization

According to Parad (1966, p. 275), a crisis is an upset in a
steady state characterized by the following phenomena: (1) a specific
and identifiable stressful event, (2) the perception of that event as
meaningful and threatening, (3) the response to the event, and (4) the
coping tasks involved in successful adaptation. Most of these points,
it should be noted, were first mentioned in the earlier works of
Lindemann and Caplan. In addition, it has already been mentioned that

during the early 1960's crisis theorists such as Rapoport (1962a) and
Bloom (1963) began to emphasize that the identification of the
precipitating event that led to the crisis was most important. In
Parad's definition of a crisis, he identifies an important concept
that earlier authors did not discuss as well. This is the concept
that the event precipitating the crisis must be perceived by the person
as a stressful situation before it becomes a crisis. Lindemann (1944)
observed this phenomenon when he studied the crisis reactions of
victims in the Coconut Grove nightclub fire. According to Lindemann,
some of the victims and their relatives did not consider the fire a
disaster but more of an act of providence. Consequently, they did not
experience the same degree of bereavement as most of the people
involved in the fire.

Like Rapoport, Parad (1960, 1962, 1968, 1971) refers to the
different stages of a crisis and acknowledges that he borrowed much
of his conceptual framework from Lindemann and Caplan. For example,
Parad (1971, p. 198) states that when a stressful event becomes a crisis
there is a period of disequilibrium in which the individual is both
vulnerable to further breakdown as well as amenable to therapeutic
influence. This is because a crisis signifies a "turning point"
requiring the use of new coping mechanisms. If these new coping
mechanisms are not found during the six to eight week period that
marks a crisis reaction, the individual may suffer irreparable emotional
and mental damage.

In his 1966 publication entitled "The Use of Time-Limited Crisis
Intervention in Community Mental Health Programming", Parad discusses

a concept of crisis that was admittedly influenced by Lindemann's
earlier advances in preventive psychiatry. This is the belief that
during a crisis a person may become a pathogenic agent or a carrier
of emotional ill health. Stated another way, a person in crisis may
have a damaging effect on the emotional health of family members,
relatives, close friends, and other significant people in his life.
In the next chapter, the writer will discuss how Jacobsen (1968) uses
this very concept in his treatment model for families in crisis.

In Parad's (1960, 1962, 1968, 1971) various publications and
articles, he has not discussed the different types of crisis reactions.
However, in his 1960 publication that he co-authored with Caplan he
does present a brief conceptualization of a family in crisis. This
conceptualization is not as clear, in the writer's opinion, as the
concepts Hill (1958) presented in an earlier article. In fact, most
of Parad's work with families in crisis deals with a brief framework
of how a family deals with stress in terms of their life-style,
problem-solving mechanisms, and need-response pattern.

Treatment Conceptualization

In discussing the initial phase of treatment, Parad (1966, p.
280) begins by stating that treatment is usually offered on a flexible
basis, beginning with frequent office and home interviews during the
crisis period and tapering off with less frequent contacts when a new
equilibrium appears to have been restored. More specifically, Parad
(1971, p. 200) believes that during this initial contact, which seldom
covers more than the first interview, the therapist should be especially

concerned with three questions: (1) What is troubling the client?
(2) Why does he come for help now? (3) What can I do to help?

As the reader will note, this initial phase of treatment as
described by Parad includes some obvious elements of assessment,
particularly identifying the precipitating event that led to the crisis
along with understanding why the client perceives this event as a
crisis. This is why Rapoport and Parad both believe that the initial
and assessment stages of crisis intervention are inseparable. Still,
Rapoport mentions an important concept of the initial phase that Parad
does not discuss. This is communicating by word and action that the
worker will help the client resolve his crisis and overcome his feelings
of hopelessness and despair.

Like Rapoport, the treatment strategies proposed by Parad call
for an active role by the therapist. Specifically, Parad (1971, p. 201)
emphasizes that the worker's interventive efforts are designed (1) to
cushion the impact of the stressful event by immediate or emergency
emotional-environmental first aid and (2) to strengthen the person in
his coping and integrative struggles through on-the-spot therapeutic
clarification and guidance during the crisis. But how is this immediate
first aid implemented and sustained by the therapist? Unfortunately,
much of what Parad (1966, p. 280) suggests the therapist should do is
shrouded in esoteric terminology like positive controlled transference,
disciplined use of active techniques of confrontation, and helping the
client to solve problems within a period of time easily encompassed by
the client's ego span. Parad does not clarify these concepts but leaves
the impression that practitioners should somehow infer what he means.

In all fairness to Parad, credit must be given him for including under his discussion of treatment strategies a number of important concepts that many other crisis theorists have either overlooked or neglected. These crisis concepts deal with administrative procedures that can help to ensure that an agency dealing in crisis intervention does offer these services. Among other guidelines, Parad (1971, p. 201) believes these administrative procedures should include:

1. The elimination of waiting lists.

2. The avoidance of complex intake screening assuring that treatment will be simultaneous with diagnosis.

3. The development of an open door policy for those who may require further services when faced with new crisis.

4. The use of a built-in policy of preplanned follow-up interviews to provide feedback about the effectiveness of services.

In Part III of this study, the writer will show how many of these proposed administrative procedures are characteristic of crisis-oriented agencies.

Parad's administrative procedures further refine the nature of the client-worker agency relationship in crisis intervention. In particular this is true of the agency role in treatment. The client-worker relationship is less clear. For instance, in his writings Parad does not deal with the importance of the client and therapist working together on specific psychological tasks in resolving the crisis. The reader will remember that this was an important part of Rapoport's treatment model. Notwithstanding, Parad fails to mention the importance of psychological tasks in crisis intervention.

Finally, in assessing treatment outcome, Parad stresses the

importance of preplanned follow-up interviews to help assess if the crisis was resolved successfully. In addition, these follow-up interviews serve as a safeguard in case the client needs more help. Yet in discussing when treatment should be terminated, Parad is not very clear. In fact, he offers no criteria to determine when termination is appropriate other than the assumption that in six to eight weeks most crises are usually resolved for better or for worse.

Relationship to other Theories

Parad does not discuss how his conceptual framework of crisis intervention is related to other theories. Yet in reviewing his (1966) article on "The Use of Time-Limited Crisis Intervention in Community Mental Health Programming", there are some obvious references to other theoretical frameworks. To begin with, he states that crisis treatment places special attention on a positive controlled transference. Transference is not, of course, a crisis term but originated in Freud's theory of psychoanalysis. Next, Parad mentions that crisis intervention incorporates techniques of confrontation, advice-giving, and anticipatory guidance. In the writer's opinion, these concepts are very similar to the psychosocial theory of casework as developed by theorists such as Richmond, Garrett, Hamilton, and Hollis. Finally, Parad states that crisis treatment centers on a strong commitment by the worker in helping the client solve problems within a period of time easily encompassed by the client's ego span. This, of course, incorporates the work of ego psychologists such as Hartman, Rado, and Erikson.

In conclusion, it is obvious that much of Parad's conceptual framework of crisis intervention is related to other theories of human behavior. Particularly is this true of his use of psychoanalytic concepts like transference and their adaptation by theorists of psycho-social casework. In addition, Parad's administrative procedures for crisis-oriented agencies are undoubtedly affected by his association with the Wellesley Human Relations Center and their concern for preventive community mental health planning.

Empirical Validation

Like Lindemann, Caplan, and Rapoport, Parad presents little empirical evidence of the effectiveness of crisis intervention. In his first article co-authored with Caplan, Parad (1960) presents a brief framework for studying families in crisis. This framework was in part the result of a research study that involved observing and interviewing families in crisis. Yet in reporting the results of the research, Parad used only one case study to describe the crisis framework and excluded any empirical data on the nature of the sample, the type of treatment given, and other important evaluation concerns.

This absence of empirical evidence was continued in Parad's (1965b, 1966, 1968) subsequent articles. In his 1971 publication, however, Parad (1971, p. 200) mentions that in a descriptive study of 1,656 cases of planned short-term crisis-oriented treatment, Libbie and Parad found that if the clinician's impressions are used as a yardstick, two-thirds of the crisis cases showed improvement. Three-fourths of the client's themselves perceived they had been helped. This research, however, has some obvious limitations. To begin with, no attempt was made to describe the crisis treatment received by the clients. Without this information, it is difficult to ascertain if crisis techniques were even used. In addition, the research reflects possible clinician and client bias because their impressions are used to evaluate treatment outcome.

In conclusion, it can be said that Parad like the previous crisis theorists discussed adds little empirical evidence that crisis intervention is effective. Subjectively, all crisis theorists seem to feel they are using a most effective treatment model. Yet when it comes to solid, unbiased empirical evidence, this claim is difficult to substantiate.

Unresolved Issues and Problems

Parad (1971, pp. 201-203) feels that the crucial task facing crisis intervention is to build up a cumulative body of knowledge rather than settle for the largely repetitive one it now has. Therefore, Parad believes that exploratory clinical action research should be conducted in the following areas:

1. Criteria for intervention.

2. The client's perception of the precipitating stressful event.

3. Whether and why the worker and client think there is a crisis and how serious it is.

4. The goals of treatment in specific rather than global terms.

5. The client's and the worker's perception of the time dimension.

6. Types of treatment techniques used.

7. How the worker and the client perceive outcome both
at the time of termination and at prearranged time
intervals following intervention.

In the writer's opinion, this statement focuses on the more
important needs prerequisite to the further refinement of crisis theory
and practice. It will be noted that over half of Parad's research
recommendations deal with treatment strategies and evaluation. This,
it would seem, is for a good reason. For too long, crisis theorists
have been focusing on the symptomatology of crisis reactions to the
neglect of treatment strategies and evaluation. All in all, these
research projects evaluating the nature of crisis reactions have added
little to the pioneering work of Lindemann and Caplan. This is what
Parad is referring to when he stresses that crisis intervention must
"build up a cumulative body of knowledge rather than settle for the
largely repetitive one it now has [p. 201]".

Conclusion

In the final analysis, most of what Parad conceptualizes as
crisis intervention theory and practice is a further refinement of
Lindemann and Caplan's earlier findings, particularly around the
symptomatology of crisis reactions. Yet like Rapoport, Parad did
transcend this focus on crisis reactions by beginning to explore
specific crisis treatment strategies. In so doing, he reinforced
such concepts as the client's need for immediate service and the
treatment goal of returning the client to at least his pre-crisis
level of functioning. In addition, Parad developed a number of
administrative procedures that need to be an essential part of any

crisis intervention agency if effective services are to be given to clients in crisis.

CHAPTER VI

GERALD F. JACOBSEN

Introduction

The writer has included a review of Gerald F. Jacobsen's

conceptual framework of crisis intervention primarily because he

presents a novel way of looking at crisis treatment. In comparison

with the other major theorists of crisis intervention, Jacobsen has

not yet developed as extensive a conceptual framework, although he

has considered carefully the issues of treatment strategies and

evaluation.

Crisis Conceptualization

Jacobsen (1968) conceptualizes the term "crisis" by quoting

directly from the earlier works of Caplan:

> A crisis is provoked when a person faces an
> obstacle to important life goals that is, for a
> time, insurmountable through the utilization of
> customary methods of problem-solving. A period
> of disorganization ensues, a period of upset,
> during which many different abortive attempts
> at solution are made. Eventually some kind of
> adaptation is achieved which may or may not be
> in the best interest of that person or his
> fellows [p. 338].

In addition, Jacobsen stresses that a crisis results only if the

individual experiencing the crisis has not previously developed coping

mechanisms to deal with the situation. These views of crisis, of course, are identical to those of Lindemann and Caplan.

In referring to the different stages of a crisis, Jacobsen also incorporates the earlier work of Lindemann and Caplan. For example, Jacobsen (1968, p. 338) feels a crisis reaction follows these three stages: (1) a period of disorganization precipitated by a stressful event (2) followed by a period of upset leading to increase tension (3) that leads to emergency problem-solving mechanisms when traditional patterns of coping fail. Then, like Caplan, Rapoport, and Parad, Jacobsen confirms that within six to eight weeks the crisis is usually resolved for better or for worse.

Unlike the other major crisis theorists, Jacobsen does not classify different crises according to Erikson's earlier framework of adaptational and situational crises. Instead, Jacobsen (1968, p. 338) states that any classification of crises must include references to the social, intrapsychic, and somatic factors involved or the biopsycho-social field. This sounds very much like Hollis' (1964) psychosocial approach to casework in which she emphasizes the person-in-the-situation. According to Jacobsen, the social factor of crisis refers to any role changes or other alterations in the interpersonal behavior. In terms of Erikson's classification system, this corresponds with situational or accidental crises such as illness, death, unemployment, and other situations that involve a role change. Jacobsen's intrapsychic factors of crisis emphasize the changes in a previously existing equilibrium within the psychic apparatus that involve unconscious as well as conscious processes. This crisis classification corresponds with Erikson's maturational or developmental crises of birth, infancy, childhood, adolescence, etc. In discussing the somatic classification of crisis, Jacobsen refers to pathogenic grief that may result in chronic psychosomatic illnesses. Erikson does not have a crisis category that fits this description.

After reviewing Jacobsen's different categories of crisis, the writer believes that Jacobsen has drawn many of his concepts from the earlier works of Erikson. In fact, it seems that in most instances Jacobsen's concepts are an extension of Erikson's developmental theory.

Treatment Conceptualization

In discussing crisis treatment strategies, Jacobsen identifies two separate approaches, the generic and the specific, and then discusses the treatment techniques of each model. The central thesis of the generic approach to crisis treatment is that for each crisis, such as bereavement, prematurity, divorce, etc., there are certain identifiable patterns that require specific psychological tasks if the crisis is to be successfully resolved. For example, in Lindemann's (1944) study on grief reactions, he stresses the importance of "grief work" if the bereavement period is to be overcome successfully. Consequently, Lindemann (1944, p. 147) states that the following tasks have to be accomplished by the grieving client:

1. Accept the pain of bereavement.

2. Review his relationships with the deceased and become acquainted with the alterations in his own modes of emotional reaction.

3. Express sorrow and sense of loss.

4. Find an acceptable formulation of his future relationships to the deceased.

5. Verbalize his feelings of guilt and find persons around him whom he can use as "primers" for the acquisition of new patterns of conduct.

The generic approach to crisis treatment usually results in the initial and assessment stages of treatment being combined with the implementation of treatment. Jacobsen (1968) explains why this is generally the case in the following statement:

> There is no attempt to determine or assess the specific psychodynamics of the individual involved in the crisis. Rather, the focus is on the course that a particular kind of crisis characteristically follows and a corresponding treatment plan aimed toward adaptive resolution of the crisis [p. 340].

Therefore, the treatment strategy is designed to be effective for the target group as a whole and focuses on the completion of certain psychological tasks associated with the particular crisis. For example, Caplan (1965) points out that in the crisis of premature births all mothers must acknowledge that their infants' lives are in danger and prepare for that impending loss. This preparation for the child's death is only one of many psychological tasks that mothers must complete in resolving successfully the crisis of prematurity.

In implementing the treatment strategies of the generic approach, emphasis is placed on accomplishing these specific psychological tasks that are by definition clear and precise and describe what the client must do. The accomplishment of these tasks, however, requires that the client and worker engage in a mutually directed problem-solving activity. In addition, any evaluation or assessment of crisis treatment must be based on how well these psychological tasks were accomplished by the client.

In summary, the generic approach to crisis treatment provides the therapist and client with clear treatment tasks that correspond to the particular crisis. This means that little emphasis is placed on individual dynamics because the psychological tasks facing the client are the same for any other person dealing with a similar crisis. Jacobsen (1968) feels this generic treatment approach has particular merit because "it provides a rationale for a type of crisis intervention which may be carried out by persons not specifically trained in the mental health field, such as nonpsychiatric physicians, nurses, welfare workers, and so on [p. 340]".

The specific or individual approach to crisis treatment differs from the generic model in its emphasis on the clinician's professional assessment of the individual in crisis. In fact, this assessment phase which also incorporates the initial stage of treatment focuses on why the previous equilibrium or homeostasis has been disturbed and what is required to restore the balance. This individual concern for the client is reflected in Parad's (1971, p. 200) three initial questions: What is troubling the client? Why does he come for help now? What can I do to help?

Once the precipitating event has been identified, the therapist needs to assess the psychological and psychosocial processes that are influencing the client. Specifically, the therapist needs to assess why the client's normally effective patterns of coping are no longer sufficient and what can be done to enhance his coping abilities. This, of course, requires extensive knowledge and experience in assessing the psychological and psychosocial processes that are interacting with the client. Consequently, this is an inherent weakness of the individual approach to crisis treatment because many workers will not have this clinical expertise.

Jacobsen (1968) does not explain in any detail the implementation of the individual approach to crisis treatment except by saying that it is "most effectively carried out by individuals with preexisting skills in one of the mental health disciplines, who have undergone further training in the theory and practice of crisis intervention [p. 342]".

Relationship to other Theories

In Jacobsen's (1965a, 1965b, 1968, 1970) articles on crisis theory and practice, he does not discuss how crisis intervention is related to other theories of human behavior. Yet since much of what Jacobsen says appears to be d r a w n from other crisis theorists such as Lindemann and Caplan, Rapoport, and Parad, it is obvious that his model of crisis intervention also incorporates other models of social intervention including ego psychology, psychoanalysis, learning theory, etc.

Empirical Validation

Only one of Jacobsen's (1965a) articles deals in any depth with the empirical validation of crisis theory and practice. In this article entitled "Crisis Theory and Treatment Strategy", Jacobsen describes the crisis services offered by the Benjamin Rush 24-hour walk-in clinic in Los Angeles. At this center, treatment focues on the immediate problem

or crisis, rather than long-standing pathology or well established
character patterns. Still, the treatment strategy is rather sketchy
and does not clarify the specific characteristics of crisis intervention. In addition, Jacobsen offers no empirical validation of the
crisis services. Once again, this lack of empirical evidence reinforces
the need for more evaluative research in crisis intervention.

Unresolved Issues and Problems

In reviewing Jacobsen's conceptual framework of crisis theory
and practice, it is obvious that he has not developed an extensive
model of crisis intervention. What he does present is a further
refinement of earlier theorists. And like these earlier theorists,
he presents a limited model of crisis treatment, particularly with
respect to treatment strategies and evaluation. These issues remain
as some of the major problems of crisis intervention.

Yet unlike any of the other theorists mentioned, Jacobsen tries
to integrate many of the different ideas about crisis theory and
practice into a simple format that highlights the similarities and
differences of various treatment approaches. Through this format of
generic and individual approaches to crisis intervention, Jacobsen
gives the beginning student and the inexperienced worker a framework
to guide them in understanding what happens in crisis intervention.
This contribution is deemed important because it offers a way of making
more sense out of varying approaches and models of crisis theory and
practice.

Conclusion

In conclusion, much of Jacobsen's model of crisis intervention is a further refinement of earlier treatment patterns although he has made a major contribution by classifying various crisis treatment approaches into generic and individual categories. This framework is especially helpful to crisis intervention students and beginning practitioners.

CHAPTER VII

DONNA C. AGUILERA

Introduction

Donna C. Aguilera (1967, 1970a, 1970b, 1971) is a registered nurse who has written extensively during the last five years on crisis intervention. Like most crisis theorists, much of her conceptualization of crisis theory and practice reflects the earlier work of Lindemann and Caplan. Yet by clarifying and adding to the work of these earlier authors, Aguilera has developed one of the clearest models of crisis intervention.

Crisis Conceptualization

In defining a crisis situation, Aguilera (1970b) quotes directly from Caplan's definition. In an attempt to further clarify what constitutes a crisis, she again refers to Caplan and his concept of homeostasis. According to Caplan, the individual organism strives to live in a state of emotional equilibrium or homeostasis. When a crisis situation, such as an unexpected death, illness, or accident, occurs the traditional problem-solving mechanisms of the individual are not always adequate to cope effectively with the crisis. Consequently, the balance or equilibrium of the individual is upset. When this state of equilibrium is disturbed, the individual must either solve the crisis with emergency coping mechanisms or adapt to a nonsolution of the crisis. Whatever the individual does, a new state of equilibrium will usually develop within six to eight weeks that may differ markedly from the previous state of social functioning. Phrased another way, this new state of equilibrium may be higher, the same, or lower than the pre-crisis level. Therefore, a crisis period may not only result in serious emotional and mental dysfunctioning but may also improve the individual's social functioning.

Referring to the earlier work of Lindemann and Caplan, Aguilera mentions that during a crisis inner tension rises, signs of anxiety appear, and there is disorganization of function, resulting in an extended period of emotional upset. These crisis stages, however, are self-limiting and usually last from four to six weeks. Aguilera again underscores the concept that a crisis is a transitional period that represents both a danger and an opportunity for growth. In any event, the crisis outcome usually depends to a significant degree on the availability of appropriate help.

In her article on "Sociocultural Factors: Barriers to Therapeutic Intervention", Aguilera (1970a) refers to Erikson's earlier classification of crises under the categories of maturational and situational crises. These categories of crises are referred to again in Aguilera's (1970b) book on crisis intervention. For example, situational crises are described as stressful situations that often effect a person's status or life roles, i.e. illness, unemployment, accidents, etc. Maturational crises, in comparison, are part of the normal processes of growth and development and include birth, infancy, childhood, etc.

In summary, the writer feels that Aguilera's conceptualization of crisis is basically a further refinement of the earlier work of Lindemann and Caplan and some of the other crisis theorists. As such, she adds little new knowledge to the definition of a crisis or its characteristic stages and types.

Treatment Conceptualization

In discussing treatment strategies in crisis intervention, Aguilera combines the initial or study phase with the assessment stage. Consequently, she feels that the first phase of crisis practice is the assessment of the individual and his problem. According to Aguilera (1970b), this "requires the use of active focusing techniques on the part of the therapist to obtain an accurate assessment of the precipitating event and the resulting crisis that brought the individual to seek professional help [p. 16]". In other words, the initial focus of the therapist is on identifying the precipitating event that led to the crisis. During this initial contact with the client, the therapist must also assess whether the client presents a high suicidal or homocidal risk. If it is felt that the client is a danger to himself or to others, emergency hospitalization may be required.

After an accurate assessment of the precipitating event and emotional state of the client has been made, crisis intervention is planned. Aguilera emphasizes that this time-limited intervention is not designed to result in major personality changes but rather to restore the client to at least his pre-crisis level of functioning.

In order to do this, time is spent with the client discussing what
strengths he has, what coping skills he used successfully in the past
and is not presently using, and which important people in his life
might be able to give him emotional support during this time of crisis.

In referring to specific treatment strategies that can be used
in crisis treatment, Aguilera (1970b, pp. 15-17) mentions some of
Morley's (1970) suggestions. First, the client should be helped to
gain an intellectual understanding of his crisis. This is important
since many clients do not see a relationship between a hazardous
situation and the extreme discomfort they subsequently experience.
Morley feels this is best done when the therapist uses a direct
approach and describes to the client the relationship between the crisis
and his emotional state. Next, the client is helped in expressing his
present feelings toward the crisis. This is particularly crucial if
the client's tension is to be relieved so he can move on to resolving
the crisis successfully. After this emotional catharsis has occurred,
the therapist and client explore alternative ways of coping with the
crisis. Often this phase includes the identification of outside
resources, such as homemaker services, that can increase a client's
coping ability. Then after the tension abates and the client gains
more mastery of the crisis, the therapist and client move into the
final stage of anticipatory planning. Here the therapist summarizes
with the client the adaptive coping mechanisms that he has used in
dealing successfully with the crisis and explains how these coping
skills will help him deal with future crisis situations. Then the
therapist concludes by encouraging the client to return whenever he

needs help.

In summarizing the important features of crisis treatment, Aguilera (1970b, p. 16) emphasizes the following points that she and Morley developed:

1. It is essential that the therapist view the work that he is doing not as a "second-best" approach but as the treatment of choice with persons in crisis.

2. Accurate assessment of the presenting problem, not a diagnostic evaluation, is essential to an effective intervention.

3. Both the therapist and the client should keep in mind throughout the contacts that the treatment is sharply time-limited and persistently direct their energies toward the resolution of the presenting problem.

4. Dealing with material not directly related to the crisis has no place in an intervention of this kind.

5. The therapist must be willing to take an active and sometimes directive role in the intervention. The relatively slow-paced approach of more traditional treatments is inappropriate in this type of therapy.

6. Maximum flexibility of approach is encouraged. Such diverse techniques such as serving as a resource person or information giver, taking an active role in establishing liaison with other helping resources, and so forth are often appropriate in particular situations.

7. The goal toward which the treatment is striving is explicit. His energy is directed entirely toward returning the individual to at least his precrisis level of functioning.

Relationship to other Theories

In Aguilera's (1970b) opinion, the "crisis approach to therapeutic intervention has been developed only within the past few decades and is based upon a broad range of theories of human behavior, including those of Freud, Hartman, Rado, Erikson, Lindemann and Caplan [p. 2]".

For instance, Aguilera feels that Freud's principle of causality as
it related to psychic determinism led future theorists such as Erikson
and Rado to develop theories of developmental psychology. Briefly
stated, psychic determinism is Freud's concept that every act of human
behavior has its cause, or source, in the history and experience of
the individual. Hartman (1958) took this concept of psychic determinism
and developed a theory of ego psychology that attempts to explain how
the ego functions of memory, thinking, and language help the individual
respond autonomously to a changing environment.

It is clear from Aguilera's conceptual framework of crisis
theory and practice that much of what she developed is greatly influenced
by Lindemann and Caplan. However, it would be unfair to say that she
has only borrowed from these two pioneers in crisis intervention. In
fact, with the help of colleagues like Morley, Farrell, and Messick,
Aguilera has developed probably the clearest conceptualiztion of crisis
treatment.

Empirical Validation

Like most of the crisis theorists reviewed earlier, Aguilera
does not present any empirical evidence in evaluating crisis practice
other than a few case studies. These case studies, however, document
quite clearly many of the important characteristics of crisis treatment.
Case studies, however, are subject to the bias of the therapist, who
may intentionally or unintentionally distort what actually happened
in the case. With this limitation in mind, the following case study
is presented as some empirical validation of Aguilera's theory of crisis

intervention.

Briefly, Aguilera's (1970b, pp. 58-62) case study concerns
Laura and Peter G. and the crisis they faced as parents of a premature
child. In helping Laura in particular deal with this crisis, Aguilera
followed a treatment plan that focused on the following crisis tasks:

1. She must realize that she may lose the baby. This
   anticipatory grief involves a gradual withdrawal
   from the relationship already established with the
   child during the pregnancy.

2. She must acknowledge failure in her maternal function
   to deliver a full-term baby.

3. After separation from the infant due to its prolonged
   hospital stay she must resume her relationship with
   it in preparation for the infant's homecoming.

4. She must prepare herself for the job of caring for
   the baby through an understanding of its special
   needs and growth patterns.

During the first phase of treatment, the therapist at the
hospital helped both Laura and Peter explore their feelings around
the possible death of their premature son. This was done with great
reluctance by both parents who continued to deny the fact that their
premature infant was in any danger. This denial continued until the
child was finally brought home from the hospital and both parents
realized that this small infant needed special attention if he was to
survive. At this stage in the crisis treatment, the therapist helped
Laura and Peter with their fears of caring for the infant. This was
partially done by educating both parents in the special needs of
premature infants and how, as parents, they could best meet those needs.
Soon, Laura and Peter felt more comfortable about meeting the needs of
their premature son and within a few weeks they were functioning much

better. Later follow-up visits showed that Laura and Peter had
continued to maintain their improved level of functioning.

Unresolved Issues and Problems

In the writer's opinion, the work of Aguilera and her colleagues
is helping to bring crisis intervention theory, especially the crisis
treatment aspect, to a much clearer level of conceptualization. Now
it seems that the next task is evaluating the effectiveness of these
models of crisis treatment as they are operationalized into practice
by experienced clinicians. Aguilera has started this evaluation
through the use of extensive case studies that tend to support her
treatment strategies. Yet for this research to be more valid, improved
research methodology with controls for such factors as possible
therapist bias in evaluation is needed. More will be said on this
point and other methodological questions later in the study.

It is important to note that by further crystallizing the
practice components of crisis intervention, Aguilera has faced one
of the most difficult problems impeding the future development of
crisis theory and practice. This, of course, concerns the conceptualization of crisis practice to the extent that its stages of treatment
can be clearly identified and followed by therapists. With this goal
partially accomplished, Aguilera and other crisis theorists can begin
to identify which crisis treatment strategies are effective with
different types of crises.

Conclusion

This concludes the review of the more important crisis theorists and practitioners. In the chapter that follows, some of the more important contributions other theorists have made to the growth and development of crisis intervention will be analyzed.

CHAPTER VIII

OTHER THEORISTS

Introduction

In the preceding chapters, the contributions of the more
prominent crisis theorists have been presented and discussed. The
following chapter will analyze the more important contributions of
lesser known crisis writers.

Crisis Conceptualization

In conceptualizing the crisis concept, many theorists (Cohen and
Walder, 1971; LaSor and Strickler, 1970; Morley, 1970; Paul, 1966a;
Rusk, 1971) refer directly to Caplan's earlier definition. For example,
LaSor and Strickler (1970) quote Caplan by saying that a crisis is a
"relatively short period of psychological disequilibrium in a person
who confronts a hazardous circumstance that for him constitutes an
important problem which he can for the time being neither escape nor
solve with his customary problem-solving resources [p. 301]". Other
theorists (Bloom, 1963; Bonstedt, 1970; Brandon, 1970; Kaplan, 1968)
either borrow directly from Caplan's definition of crisis or acknowledge
that his definition is the basis for the one they have developed.

Yet some of these theorists add some important insights to the
earlier crisis concepts of Lindemann and Caplan. Sifneos (Golan, 1969,

pp. 390-393), for example, identifies four components of an emotional crisis: (1) the hazardous event, (2) the vulnerable state, (3) the precipitating factor, and (4) the state of active crisis. This conceptual framework of the component parts of a crisis is interesting because Sifneos makes a distinction between the hazardous event and the precipitating factor. According to his framework, the hazardous event leads to the crisis while the precipitating factor is that final event or circumstance that makes the hazardous event unbearable and results in the crisis. This corresponds with some of Lindemann's (1944) earlier findings, particularly the finding that some people have the capacity to endure a number of hazardous events without experiencing a crisis reaction. Yet these same people are often thrown into a state of crisis by a precipitating factor that is not nearly as severe as the earlier hazardous events. This interaction of hazardous event and precipitating factor is reflected in the age-old cliche of "the straw that broke the camel's back". Sifneos' interactive concept of hazardous event and precipitating factor gives a further explanation of why some people have a higher tolerance to certain crisis situations only to finally succumb when a less serious event occurs.

In Schulberg and Sheldon's (1968) publication on "The Probability of Crisis and Strategies for Preventive Intervention", they incorporate those concepts of a crisis reaction into a conceptual framework designed to predict how an individual, family, group, community, or even nation might react to a future crisis situation. In trying to develop a probability formula for a crisis, Schulberg and Sheldon (1968, pp. 554-555) believe it is necessary to consider at least three factors:

(1) the probability that a hazardous event will occur, (2) the
probability that an individual will be exposed to this event, and
(3) the vulnerability of the individual to the event. Stated in
equation form, this probability formula is:

P crisis = f(hazardous event X exposure X vulnerability)

In other words, the probability of a crisis situation occurring because
of a hazardous event is a function (or result) of the interaction
between the hazardous event, the exposure of the individual to the
event, and the vulnerability of the individual, group, etc. to that
event.

This conceptual framework for predicting crisis reactions
appears to have great merit, particularly in assessing what might
happen to a neighborhood or community if a certain hazardous event,
such as sudden unemployment, occurs. This is important because with
this predictive knowledge courses of action can be agreed upon before-
hand and then put into action immediately after the crisis occurs.
This would be especially valuable in emergency disaster planning.

As the reader will remember, the concept of homeostasis, or
the individual's psychological and physiological attempts to maintain
a dynamic equilibrium, is an important part of Caplan's definition and
description of a crisis reaction. Taplin (1971) believes these "homeostatic theories lose usefulness because their theoretical core, the
homeostatic balance, cannot effectively characterize essential aspects
of human behavior, such as growth, development, change, and actualiza-
tion [p. 14]". The writer does not agree with this criticism, however,

because it ignores Rado's (Aguilera, 1970, p. 3) concept of adaptational psychodynamics, which is the foundation of homeostasis and describes the adaptation of the human organism and subsequent personality development. Moreover, the concept of homeostasis and its relationship to psychological and physiological growth and development had earlier been explicated by Cannon (1932) in his book The Wisdom of the Body.

With respect to the different stages of a crisis, most of the authors (Bonstedt, 1970; Brandon, 1970; Forer, 1963; Kaplan, 1968; Morley, 1970; LaSor and Strickler, 1970; Rusk, 1971) refer directly to Lindemann (1944) and Caplan's (1964) earlier works. Brandon (1970, p. 628), for instance, restates Caplan's four stages of crisis: (1) an initial rise in tension due to the precipitating event, (2) the lack of success in dealing with this rise in tension with customary problem-solving mechanisms, (3) the further rise in tension that elicits emergency problem-solving methods, and (4) the threat of severe emotional disorder if some equilibrium is not restored. Hill (1949, 1958), apparently working independently from Lindemann and Caplan, developed his own stages of crisis reactions involving individuals and families. According to Hill (1949, pp. 13-14), the course of an individual or family's reaction to a crisis follows a roller coaster pattern. First upon meeting a crisis, the individual is numbed by the blow. Then as the full impact of the situation forces the individual to face the reality of the crisis, there follows a downward slump in behavior wherein the individual often becomes confused, disoriented, and helpless. After this brief period of disorganization, the individual attempts to recover from the crisis by using emergency coping mechanisms.

If these fail, the tension created by the crisis can result in marked depression. Usually, however, some level of equilibrium is established by these emergency procedures. Still, this new level of equilibrium may be the same, higher, or lower than the pre-crisis level of functioning.

Sachs (1968, p. 113) has taken these concepts and, using Hill's earlier illustration, developed the following diagram of a crisis reaction:

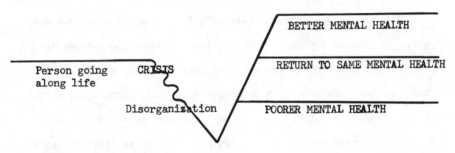

This illustration shows that a crisis first leads to a period of disorganization. Yet based on how the individual copes with the crisis, the eventual outcome may find the individual in an even better state of functioning. Which state at outcome finally occurs, of course, is often the result of the kind of help a person receives from others during the crisis. Most crisis theorists (Lindemann, 1944; Caplan, 1964; Rapoport, 1970; Parad, 1966; Aguilera, 1970b) state that effectively used techniques of crisis intervention are designed to return the individual to at least his pre-crisis level of functioning and hopefully even improve it. This illustration by Hill and Sachs is a valuable tool in elucidating this concept.

In defining the characteristics of different types of crises,

none of the authors (Kaplan, 1962; Klemme, 1970; Malamud, 1927;
Rogers, 1970) added much to the knowledge base of crisis intervention.
In fact, almost all of them point to the pioneering work of Erikson
(1956), particularly in defining and describing developmental and
situational crises. Hill (1949, 1958), however, has taken some of
Erikson's ideas and developed a conceptual framework to describe
different types of family crises. According to Hill's (1958, pp. 142-
147) framework, family crises are either intra-family or extra-family
in nature and fall under the following categories: (1) dismemberment
only, (2) assession only, (3) demoralization only, (4) demoralization
plus dismemberment or assession. The category "dismemberment only"
would include such crises as the death of a child, spouse, or parent
while the category of "assession only" includes crisis situations like
an unwanted pregnancy, some adoptions, or an aged relative coming to
live with a family. Crises that cause demoralization include nonsupport,
infidelity, alcoholism, and drug abuse while divorce and suicide can
have a demoralizing and dismemberment affect on the family. In the
writer's judgment, Hill's description of families in crisis gives
further understanding to the nature and characteristics of the crisis
reaction.

Treatment Conceptualization

Most of the crisis theorists (Bonstedt, 1970; Brandon, 1970;
Kaplan, 1968; Morley, 1970; LaSor and Strickler, 1970; Rusk, 1971)
reviewed base their treatment strategies on the earlier works of
Lindemann and Caplan, Rapoport, Parad, etc. On the other hand, other

theorists (Cohen and Walder, 1971; Golan, 1969; Mc Gee, 1968; Taplin, 1971) present such abbreviated conceptualizations of crisis practice that it is extremely difficult to identify any distinguishing characteristics. Still, some crisis theorists (Brandon, 1970; Forer, 1963; Morley, 1970; Paul, 1966b; Rusk, 1971; Sachs, 1968; Schulberg and Sheldon, 1968) build on the work of earlier authors and, in many instances, add to the knowledge base of crisis treatment.

Brandon (1970) does not discuss the various stages of crisis treatment, although he does emphasize that during crisis intervention early and frequent support is needed, especially in meeting the dependency needs of the client. More specifically, he stresses that during a crisis the worker may have to complete certain tasks for the client before movement begins. For example, a husband who has just experienced the emergency hospitalization of his wife may have to contend with four or five young children and all the additional tasks his wife was doing such as washing their clothes, preparing their meals, etc. Many distraught husbands do not know where to begin and, unless close relatives are willing to help, they are left with an overwhelming task. The worker can help the husband begin to meet these pressures by suggesting or even advising the use of a home-maker service while his wife is hospitalized and even making those arrangements for the husband. This is part of what Brandon refers to when he discusses meeting the dependency needs of crisis clients.

Morley (1970, pp. 17-18), on the other hand, discusses four different levels of crisis treatment: (1) environmental manipulation, (2) general support, (3) generic approach, and (4) individual approach.

Environmental manipulation occurs when the helping person puts the
client in touch with a resource person or facility that can remove
the hazard or lessen its effect. A good example of this type of crisis
treatment would be when the helping person refers the client to the
Department of Public Assistance after he has just lost a job. This
is the type of crisis counseling that Morley feels a minister or
physician might engage in because they lack the skill and/or the time
to help the client directly. General support is listening in a non-
threatening manner and allowing the person to speak in some detail
about his problem. Again, this is the crisis counseling approach that
a minister, physician, or close friend may adopt. In contrast, the
last two crisis approaches, generic and individual, are two different
treatment models that were discussed earlier in the study by Jacobsen
(1968). Both Morley and Jacobsen define the generic approach as
helping the client resolve a crisis by accomplishing certain psychological tasks that are the same for all people dealing with the same
crisis situation. In comparison, the individual approach is based on
the premise that in resolving a crisis situation the treatment strategies
need to meet the specific needs of the individual. Unfortunately, in
presenting these four levels of crisis treatment Morley does not
develop in any depth what characterizes the different stages of
intervention, such as the initial, assessment, etc. Still, Morley's
four levels of crisis intervention offer crisis theorists a chance to
define and conceptualize their treatment models more clearly.

In Paul's (1966a, pp. 142-143) article on "Crisis Intervention",
he asserts that in crisis therapy the worker must accomplish four tasks:

1. Identify (to yourself) the precipitating event.

2. Discern (for yourself) the defensive maneuvers employed against the responses to the precipitating stress event.

3. Acquaint the client with the main (most powerful) defenses he is using against recognizing and feeling the responses.

4. Acquaint him with the precipitating event and the responses to it he is warding off.

In the writer's opinion, this step-by-step guide to crisis intervention seems to leave out clarification as to how the crisis situation is finally resolved. In fact, it seems appropriate to add a fifth task to Paul's model: Identify with the client the psychological tasks associated with resolving the crisis and work with him in completing those tasks. This approach tends to follow Morley's (1970) concept of generic crisis intervention because the worker follows the same treatment plan with all clients.

Rusk (1971) gives some additional insight on crisis treatment by saying that "the golden rule for the therapist in crisis intervention is to do for others that which they cannot do for themselves and no more [p. 251]". In order to do this, Rusk (1971, pp. 255-257) proposes four specific tactics for intervention: (1) affectual release, (2) current life focus, (3) fostering maturity, and (4) unsatisfied needs. The first tactic of affectual release encourages client expression of the most significant emotions. Rusk feels this is essential because it induces appreciation in the client and provides an opportunity for empathy on the part of the worker. The next tactic, current life focus, concentrates on the precipitating events that led to the crisis and helps the client focus on the task at hand. By fostering maturity, the

worker has the client assume as much responsibility for his treatment
as possible. This is partially accomplished by engaging the client
in identifying what psychological tasks he feels will help resolve the
crisis. Finally, the worker needs to explore with the client his
unsatisfied needs by assessing the current life situation.

In summary, many of these crisis theorists have helped to refine
further crisis treatment, although none of them has developed a conceptual framework that describes in depth the various stages of crisis
practice. In fact, most of the crisis theorists reviewed in this
chapter have merely restated Lindemann and Caplan's earlier ideas.

Relationship to other Theories

Most crisis theorists (Brandon, 1970; Golan, 1969; Hill, 1949,
1958; LaSor and Strickler, 1970; Morley, 1970; Paul, 1966a; Taplin,
1971) fail to mention how crisis intervention is related to other
theories of human behavior and social intervention. On the other hand,
some authors discuss crisis intervention and planned short-term treatment as if they were the same model. Therefore, it is important to
determine what differences, if any, exist between crisis treatment and
planned short-term treatment. Since this is an important part of the
study, the comparison of crisis intervention with planned short-term
treatment will be delayed until Part IV of the study.

A brief word, however, can be said about the relationship of
crisis intervention to other theories. For example, crisis theory
has some of its roots in psychotherapy, particularly brief psychotherapy.
According to Bellak (1965), the therapist in brief psychotherapy "does

not have the time to wait for working-through; he must stimulate working-through. And when these basic aspects of the therapeutic process are not forthcoming, he must invent alternatives [p. 6]". This is what Lindemann (1944) did when he helped the victims of bereavement accomplish certain tasks that he felt would facilitate their recovery. Bellak then goes on to say that brief psychotherapy is to be accomplished in the short range of one to six interviews. Again, this time limit is also characteristic of crisis intervention.

However, it would be an oversight to say that crisis intervention is just an outgrowth of brief psychotherapy because there are some fundamental differences. According to most crisis theorists, the worker in crisis practice is much more active than in brief psycho-therapy. This is particularly true in conveying to the client a sense of hope that is reinforced by letting the client know that as he accomplishes certain psychological tasks the crisis will be resolved. In addition, crisis workers often manipulate the environment in helping the client resolve his crisis. It also seems that crisis intervention is more present oriented than brief psychotherapy because it is based on the assumption that before the crisis occurred most clients were normally functioning individuals. In other words, crisis intervention does not focus on past pathology like traditional and brief psychotherapy.

In conclusion, the writer would borrow Rapoport's (1970, p. 267) phrase and say that crisis intervention is a new synthesis of earlier theoretical frameworks. Crisis theory is eclectic in nature and incorporates a number of different theories of human behavior that include traditional psychotherapy, brief psychotherapy, and ego or developmental psychology, just to name a few.

Empirical Validation

In reviewing the available research on crisis intervention, the writer is impressed by the lack of research done on the effectiveness of crisis intervention. Still, there are some important evaluative studies that will be discussed later in Part III of the study. A few important studies, however, will be considered now. The first is Bloom's (1963) research on the "Definitional Aspects of the Crisis Concepts". Briefly, the purpose of Bloom's study was to determine if highly skilled crisis theorists and clinicians could agree on what circumstances constitute a crisis. In order to do this, he constructed fourteen brief case histories that described a single stressful event in the life of a fictional character named Mr. Jones. Each case history was made as realistic as possible and contained information on (a) the awareness or lack of awareness of a precipitating event, (b) the rapidity of the onset of the discomfort, (c) presence or absence of internal discomfort, (d) external evidence of behavioral disruption on the part of the presumed victim of the crisis, and (e) rapidity of resolution of the conflict. After administering the case histories to crisis theorists and clinicians at the Harvard School of Public Health, Bloom found that the judgment of crisis is made significantly more often when there is a known precipitating event. In fact, Bloom found that judgments of crisis are particularly hard to make when the precipitating event is unknown.

Bloom's findings are deemed extremely important because they

reinforce the importance of identifying and dealing with the precipitating event in crisis intervention. All of the major crisis theorists
(Lindemann, 1944; Caplan, 1964; Rapoport, 1970; Parad, 1970; Aguilera,
1970b) regard the identification of the precipitating event as the
beginning phase of crisis practice. Bloom's research lends additional
support to the importance of identifying the precipitating event.
In fact, it seems that if a recent precipitating event cannot be
identified by the client crisis intervention treatment should not
be used. This point will be considered further in the study.

In addition to Bloom's (1963) study of the crisis concept,
there are a number of other theorists (Cowen, 1972; Krause, 1968;
Lindenthal, 1970; Meyers, et. al., 1971; Sifneos, 1960; Smith, 1970;
Turner, 1966) who studied various aspects of crisis intervention.
For instance, Krause (1968) studied the occurrence of crisis in a
rehabilitation center for the severely disturbed. Among his other
findings, Krause noted that crisis situations occur most frequently
at the time and place of greatest relative deprivation and interpersonal
anomie. In addition, severely disturbed patients usually experience
one crisis after another because their coping skills are grossly
deficient. Meyers, Lindenthal, and Pepper (1971) did a similar study
designed to show the possible relationship between the occurrence of
life crises and the current social functioning of a sample of New Haven,
Connecticut residents. In their findings, they report that the greater
the degree of impairment in the resident sample, the more likely that
the individuals have experienced at least one crisis in the year before
the interview. In fact, nearly one-half of the sample evaluated as very

impaired had reported three or more crises during the past year.

These studies reflect the potential danger inherent in any crisis situation. Some people seem to be able to resolve crisis situations by themselves or with the help of close friends or relatives. Yet unresolved crises tend to weaken the coping skills of others and increase their vulnerability to further emotional and mental impairment. Consequently, if crisis situations are treated effectively, they can help an individual to resolve his immediate problem while at the same time promoting his future development.

In conclusion, the implications of a few selected empirical studies in crisis intervention have been considered. Again, it should be stressed that theorists have presented little empirical evidence that supports the claims of crisis theory and practice. Yet before these outcome studies are possible, more research also is needed in clarifying and specifying the nature of crisis treatment.

Unresolved Issues and Problems

In discussing the current issues and problems of crisis intervention, reference is made to Darbonne's (1968) article wherein he reviewed the current status of crisis theory, practice, and research. According to Darbonne (1968), crisis-relevant articles appear in widely scattered journals and "demonstrate little awareness of each other, of what has been written before, and of the relationship of crisis to previously explored concepts [p. 371]". To begin with, most major crisis theorists (Caplan, 1964; Rapoport, 1970; Parad, 1970; Aguilera, 1970b) base their concepts of crisis intervention on the earlier work of Lindemann (1944) and Caplan (1960, 1964). In so doing, they demonstrate considerable awareness of what has been written before. Where they falter, in the writer's judgment, is in not adding to the earlier works of Lindemann and Caplan, particularly in conceptualizing crisis treatment. All too often, these theorists continue to duplicate the treatment strategies of earlier authors, thereby limiting the continued growth of crisis treatment.

In the same article, Darbonne (1968) also states that "further refinement of the definition of the crisis concept is necessary before research on the effectiveness of crisis intervention can be undertaken [p. 373]". The writer does not agree with this statement because further refinement of the crisis concept will probably only duplicate earlier formulations. The writer feels that enough theory building has already been done in this area as attested by the works of Lindemann (1944, 1956, 1961), Caplan (1960, 1964), Hill (1949, 1958), Rapoport (1962a, 1967, 1970), and countless other crisis theorists. Crisis theorists should now devote their energies to conceptualizing and researching the nature of crisis treatment. Some theorists (Bonstedt, 1970; Kaplan, 1968; Golan, 1969) have already tried to assess the effectiveness of crisis practice although their findings are debatable since none of them presented clear conceptualizations of crisis practice.

In summary, the writer believes the future growth of crisis theory depends greatly on the expansion of the conceptualization of crisis practice. Without this new direction, crisis theorists will probably continue to research the nature of the crisis reaction, a subject about which abundant information already exists.

Conclusion

This concludes the review of the most important crisis theorists.
In summary, the writer again acknowledges the pioneering work of
Lindemann (1944, 1956, 1961) and Caplan (1960, 1964, 1965) in the
growth and development of crisis intervention theory and practice.
Lindemann and Caplan were the first theorists to study systematically
the nature of the crisis reaction and then to develop a conceptual
framework to describe it. In addition, they were the first theorists
to describe the successful treatment of a crisis reaction by identifying
the stressful event and then attempting to help the client accomplish
certain psychological tasks. Later theorists, most notably Rapoport
(1962a, 1967, 1970) and Aguilera (1967, 1970a, 1970b, 1971), further
explicated the practice of crisis intervention. Of the two theorists,
Aguilera presented the clearer conceptualization of crisis practice
although Rapoport was one of the first authors to conceptualize the
various stages of crisis practice. Even considering the contributions
of these more recent theorists, crisis intervention theory and practice
is still greatly influenced by the earlier works of Lindemann and Caplan.
In the following part entitled "Practice Areas of Crisis Intervention",
the writer will review what is currently known about crisis practice.

PART III

PRACTICE AREAS OF CRISIS INTERVENTION

CHAPTER IX

CHILDREN AND ADOLESCENTS

Introduction

Crisis intervention has been used in a variety of practice settings. After completing the review of the crisis literature, the writer found that crisis intervention practice focuses primarily on the five following areas: (1) childhood and adolescent crises, (2) mental health problems, (3) marital and family conflicts, (4) emergency hospitalization, and (5) suicide prevention. Therefore, it was decided to make these five practice areas the basis of the review of crisis practice. In addition, a sixth section was included to cover those practice areas of crisis intervention that did not correspond with any of the five preceding categories.

In discussing crisis intervention involving children, most of the authors (Baldwin, 1968; Blaufarb, 1972; Epstein, 1965; Keith-Lucas, 1969; Galdston and Hughes, 1972; Lang and Oppenheimer, 1968) focus either on child-guidance clinics or child hospitalization services. Therefore, much of the discussion of crisis intervention with children will focus on these two areas. Crisis practice with adolescents (Armsby, 1971; Bonier, 1971; Deeths, 1970; Denison, 1971; Hart, 1971; Riscalla, 1971), on the other hand, seems to deal primarily with adolescent clinics and correctional facilities for youth in trouble with the law. In addition, other authors (Bryt, 1962; Hurwitz, 1965;

Klein, 1965; Madison, 1971; Quinby, 1971) discuss children and adolescents in crisis without presenting any conceptual framework of crisis
practice. Some of their contributions will also be discussed.

Services Given

The first article written about children and crisis practice
is Rosenfeld and Caplan's (1954) study of Jewish immigrant children
entering Israel during the late 1940's and early 1950's. More
specifically, they discuss the efforts of the Lasker Mental Hygiene
Center of Hadassah in meeting the emotional and physical needs of
16,000 unaccompanied immigrant children from ages 6 to 17. As
Rosenfeld and Caplan (1954, p. 42) described the crisis services,
these children were first cared for in children's villages, residential
urban homes and schools, and as separate groups in the communal
agricultural settlements. Periodically, however, about 10 to 15 per
cent of the children were referred to the Lasker Center because of
"neurotic symptoms". It was at this stage that the crisis consultants
were involved in the treatment of the children.

Later uses of the crisis model (Baldwin, 1968; Cain, 1966;
Epstein, 1965) also incorporated the work of crisis consultants.
For example, Epstein (1965) discusses the Child and Family Services
Center in Chicago that offers substitute or supplementary child care
through the use of homemakers when agency clients and their workers
felt this was appropriate. This service was initiated and directed
by a crisis consultant who helped the worker begin appropriate crisis
procedures to assist a troubled child. Cain and Fast (1966) explain
that disturbed children are usually referred to their centers by parents

who are also experiencing a crisis. In particular, they discuss the disturbed child who is referred by the surviving parent after the other parent has committed suicide.

Turning to the crisis of childhood hospitalization, Lang and Oppenheimer (1968) and Morrisey (1964) discuss the reactions and crisis treatment of children who are suffering from a fatal illness. Both studies refer to the crisis of childhood leukemia. Galdston and Hughes (1972), on the other hand, describe a follow-up clinic for pediatric patients who have been hospitalized. According to the authors, the "clinic aims to achieve an effective transformation of an ego-alien crisis of illness and acute hospitalization into an opportunity for growth and development [p. 721]".

Shifting to adolescent crisis practice, the first series of authors (Armsby, 1971; Bonier and Koplovsky, 1971; Denison, 1971; Garrell, 1969) describe direct services offered by community centers in meeting the needs of adolescents in crisis. For instance, Armsby (1971) describes the Adolescent Unit at the Hawaii State Hospital that is designed to treat emotionally disturbed adolescents between the ages of 12 to 19. Bonier and Koplovsky (1971), on the other hand, describe a treatment plan of crisis intervention directed to 28 adolescents selected from 135 applicants to the Mc Lean Hospital Outpatient Clinic.

In other articles, Deeths (1970), Hart (1971), Riscalla (1970), and Villeponteaux (1970) describe the crisis treatment of adolescents in trouble with legal authorities. Deeths (1970), for instance, describes a crisis treatment service that incorporates the use of psychodrama with male drug users at a correctional facility in Stockton, California. In contrast, Villeponteaux (1970) discusses the Horizon House, a three-year pilot project in Charleston, South Carolina sponsored by the Junior League to help adolescents currently on probation for serious offenses.

In conclusion, this brief review gives a cursory look at some of the different crisis services directed toward children and adolescents. The next section of the study will attempt to clarify what these direct services consist of in practice.

Nature of Services

In describing the crisis services that were directed to immigrant Jewish children by the Lasker Center, Rosenfeld and Caplan (1954, pp. 42-48) do not refer specifically to crisis intervention. Yet many of the treatment concepts and strategies they present reflect a working knowledge of crisis theory and practice. To begin with, it will be recalled that these disturbed immigrant children were referred to the Lasker Center by the staff of communal agricultural settlements. In the initial and assessment stage of treatment, the crisis consultant is invited by the staff to come to the communal settlement and discuss the child's problem with his instructor. During this initial and assessment stage of treatment, the consultant discusses with the instructor those aspects of the child's behavior that appear disturbing. After this is completed, the consultant speaks with as many people as possible who deal with the child to supplement the perceptions previously shared by the child's instructor.

Having completed this stage of treatment, the consultant again meets with the instructor and helps him deal more effectively with the child. In constructing treatment strategies, the consultant first identifies with the instructor the nature of the problem. For example, it was explained to one instructor that a child's constant demands for removal from the settlement area is really a means of finding reassurance that he is loved and wanted. With this interpersonal dynamic in mind, the instructor was then helped to develop tasks that he could initiate in helping the boy feel more accepted. By focusing on these tasks, the boy's crisis was resolved within a two-week period.

Although the above is a sketchy conceptualization of crisis intervention, a few important ideas emerge. First of all, this study describes how the crisis consultant works with an instructor who then assumes the major treatment responsibility for the boy. The same crisis approach was used on February 9, 1971 when crisis consultants (Blaufarb and Levine, 1972, pp. 17-19) talked on the phone with over 800 parents due to the California earthquake. These consultants could not begin to treat the children by themselves anymore than Rosenfeld and Caplan could help 2,000 emotionally disturbed immigrant children. Instead, Blaufarb and Levine identified with the parents by phone the specific nature of the crisis. For most parents, it was their children's incessant crying and fear of going to sleep by themselves. Having identified with the parents that the crisis had been precipitated by the earthquake, the crisis consultants designed with the parents certain tasks they could accomplish in resolving their children's crises. One task was sharing with their children their own fear of what had happened and then reassuring the children that the earthquake had stopped and

everything was fine. Assuming this air of calmness and confidence,
the parents were better able to help their children get back to normal.
In summary, the above two studies incorporate the following points of
crisis treatment:

1. Identification of the precipitating stress.

2. Discussion of feelings concerning the crisis event.

3. Identifying with the client tasks that would be
   helpful in resolving the crisis.

4. Helping the client accomplish these crisis tasks.

These strategies of crisis practice are very similar to Berlin's
(1970) crisis work with children in a child-guidance center. In fact,
in helping the family and the child deal with a crisis situation,
Berlin (1970, p. 598) believes the worker should seek answers to the
following questions:

1. What is the crisis?

2. Whom does it affect?

3. Why is it disorganizing?

4. What were the individual's or family's resources and
   plans for coping with it prior to intervention?

5. What are the ego strengths to be mobilized?

6. How can one involve these individuals in their own
   behalf?

7. What are the specific tasks to be carried out to help
   resolve or reduce the crisis?

The above is one of the most complete treatment outlines presented by
any of the crisis theorists who discuss their work with children and
adolescents. In fact, the outline is quite similar to the ones proposed
by Rapoport (1970), Parad (1970), and Aguilera (1970b). Unfortunately,

Berlin does not continue his discussion of treatment strategies much
further. He does, however, include a brief case study of a 14-year
old boy whose sudden psychotic crisis was resolved by involving him
and his parents in certain therapeutic tasks such as teaching Fred
how to drive and going fishing with him. Through the accomplishment
of these tasks, Fred broke out of his depression and psychotic behavior
patterns.

Of all the publications reviewed on crisis intervention with
children, Baldwin (1968, pp. 28-30) presents one of the most complete
conceptualizations of crisis practice. In her paper, she describes
short-term crisis intervention practice at the Greater Lawrence
Guidance Center in Lawrence, Massachusetts. Serving a population of
150,000, the Greater Lawrence Guidance Center is the only child guidance
resource in the area. In the initial phase of treatment, the clinical
focus is on identifying what has happened to precipitate this request
for help. During this initial stage, the worker needs to investigate
what environmental events and emotional factors have recently occurred
to upset the equilibrium of the child's coping mechanisms. In other
words, during the initial phase of crisis treatment the worker involves
the client in identifying the precipitating event. This is done with
the child and his parents in individual and joint interviews.

Since identifying the precipitating event involves assessment,
Baldwin feels that the initial and assessment phases of crisis practice
are one in the same. During this joint phase of treatment, the worker
explores with the client why his traditional patterns of coping are
not sufficient in meeting this crisis. This exploration also gives the

client the opportunity to express how he is feeling about the crisis. In fact, Baldwin uses this exploration in the joint interview to develop a sense of partnership with the child and his parents.

As the client and his parents discuss individually and jointly their feelings around the crisis, the worker gives them calm assurance that this type of crisis is difficult for most people but that solutions are available. At this point, the treatment strategy becomes one of determining what specifically can be done to resolve the crisis. For example, the author gives the case illustration of Ruth, a $12\frac{1}{2}$-year old girl referred to the clinic because of hyperventilation. By exploring what had happened prior to the onset of symptoms, the worker was able to discover that her hyperventilation began shortly after the family became extremely concerned over Ruth's older sisters dangerous pregnancy condition. In response to the crisis, Ruth's mother became agitated and fearful and Ruth followed her example. By discussing the fear that surrounded this crisis, the worker helped Ruth and her parents resolve the problem. In fact, contact with Ruth and her family was terminated four weeks later when Ruth was no longer hyperventilating.

Studies on crisis intervention with adolescents will now be considered. Bonier and Koplovsky (1971, pp. 437-438) discuss treatment of 28 adolescents at the Mc Lean Hospital Outpatient Clinic and in describing their treatment plan, they present a brief practice model. To begin with, each adolescent is seen initially by a psychiatrist in an extensive interview designed to elicit information concerning diagnosis, precipitating factors, and the role of other family members in the crisis. Then each adolescent is assigned to a social worker for further treatment which consists of four treatment interviews within a one-month period. In general, the crisis treatment focuses upon the precipitating stress and how it can be resolved. This, of course, is a very general framework of crisis practice with adolescents, although it does give some indication of how crisis treatment can be used in a time-limited team approach.

In his article entitled "The Adolescent Crisis Team: An Experiment in Community Crisis Intervention", Armsby (1971) describes the use of the Adolescent Crisis Team at the Hawaii State Hospital. Basically, this crisis team "is designed to respond to requests for admission to the Adolescent Unit by focusing on the system in distress instead of allowing that system to label the adolescent as 'sick' and extrude him into the hospital [p. 735]". This is accomplished by referring all requests for adolescent admission to the crisis team coordinators. If they determine the adolescent is suicidal or danger-ously psychotic, he is brought to the inpatient unit immediately. If his condition is not that grave, the crisis coordinators assign a two-man team (usually a social worker and an aide) to meet with the adolescent at the scene of the crisis. In other words, the initial phase of treatment begins as the crisis team goes to meet the adolescent who is generally at his home. They arrive as soon as possible and use the heightened anxiety in encouraging expression of feeling. In fact, most of the treatment strategy centers around action-oriented psycho-drama techniques that are used in aiding the family members to share their feelings honestly and directly with each other. This is done for two to eight sessions and then the crisis team follows-up with the family in three months, six months, and one-year periods.

This treatment approach of Armsby is interesting from a number of standpoints. First of all, it is one of only a few approaches or strategies that encourages visiting the crisis client in his home during the height of stress. This appears to have substantial merit because it emphasizes giving immediate help to the crisis client in the context of his social milieu and involves other members of his family. This is important because they can give him support and encouragement; but even more significant, they are often important elements in the crisis. In addition, helping a crisis client and his family members share their honest feelings can be a valuable tool in crisis intervention, especially in opening new channels of family communication. This expression of honest feeling can also be used in helping the client and his family identify the precipitating stress, express their feelings around the crisis, and then decide and carry through as a family what tasks they will focus on in resolving the crisis.

The other adolescent studies (Deeths, 1970; Hart, 1971; Riscalla, 1970; Villeponteaux, 1970) suffer more or less from unclear conceptual- izations of crisis practice. For example, Hart's (1971) crisis treatment strategies for girls institutionalized in a correctional school emphasizes that full-time concern for the girls is essential because they constant- ly seek reassurance. Yet Hart fails to mention how this is done. In addition, he offers no description or explanation of the various stages of crisis intervention and how crisis treatment is implemented by the worker. Villeponteaux (1970) is equally confusing in defining crisis

treatment, particularly the implementation of treatment strategies.
Riscalla (1970), on the other hand, is a little more clear about her
crisis treatment. For example, she states that most institutionalized
adolescent offenders are reluctant to face their problems. Consequently, the thrust of crisis treatment needs to lessen that resistance and
make the adolescent more amenable to the worker's advice. This is
somewhat like crisis treatment but only to the extent that more specific
tasks, like advice, are used in treatment. Still, it falls considerably short of crisis intervention because the client is not actively
involved in his own treatment. In addition, Riscalla fails to mention
how the worker can best overcome the resistance of these adolescent
offenders.

In summary, the writer feels that a few of the authors (Armsby,
1971; Baldwin, 1968; Berlin, 1971; Blaufarb and Levine, 1972; Rosenfeld
and Caplan, 1954) who describe crisis practice with children and
adolescents present fairly clear conceptual frameworks of crisis treatment, although none of them are as clear as those of Rapoport (1970),
Parad (1970), or Aguilera (1970b). Unfortunately, the other authors
present sketchy theories of crisis practice. In fact, the only criterion
that associates most of them with crisis intervention is the fact that
the client came for help experiencing a crisis reaction.

Service Evaluation

Most of the crisis practitioners (Baldwin, 1968; Berlin, 1970;
Blaufarb and Levine, 1972; Epstein, 1965; Galdston and Hughes, 1972;
Keith-Lucas, 1969; Rosenfeld and Caplan, 1954; Stein, 1970) reviewed

used case study material to document the effectiveness of crisis practice with children and adolescents. Many of these case studies (Epstein, 1965; Keith-Lucas, 1969; Rosenfeld and Caplan, 1954; Stein, 1970) were so brief that it was often difficult to tell whether or not the worker was using crisis practice. On the other hand, some of these case studies (Baldwin, 1968; Berlin, 1970; Galdston and Hughes, 1972) were extremely well documented and verified that crisis practice was being followed.

Those empirical studies that appear to be the most important were conducted by Baldwin (1968) and Berlin (1970). This judgment is based on two reasons. First of all, both authors presented clear conceptual frameworks of crisis practice that identified and explained in some detail what generally happens in the initial, assessment, and treatment phases of crisis intervention. This is important because before researchers can evaluate the success or failure of a treatment model they must be able to state clearly what characterizes the treatment strategy. In addition, they need to make sure that clinicians use the treatment model properly. In the writer's judgment, the case examples presented by these two authors describe the more important points of crisis treatment. This is especially true of identifying with the client the nature of the precipitating stress, helping him express his feelings around the crisis, and identifying tasks that he can accomplish in resolving the problem successfully.

Still, both studies are subject to possible clinician bias because it is the worker who evaluates the final treatment outcome. A more valid approach would have been to use other researchers not

associated with the case in the final evaluation. In addition, criteria
to measure the effectiveness of crisis treatment such as task accomplishment or a before-after psychological test could have been defined before
treatment began and then used as part of the treatment evaluation.
Many research studies (Grey and Dermody, 1972; Fischer, 1973) suffer
because of similar methodological problems. In comparison with other
outcome studies, these two by Baldwin and Berlin are fairly good.

The empirical studies on crisis practice with adolescents are much
less exact than those studies on children with a few exceptions. One of
these exceptions is Armsby's (1971) research on the Adolescent Crisis
Team at the Hawaii State Hospital. Through the use of follow-up
interviews, Armsby was able to assess some of the long-term effects
of crisis treatment. Of the 106 families treated by the crisis team,
74 (70 per cent) were still together as family units six-months later.
In addition, the mean score of family functioning for all treated
families had significantly improved based on the 20-item Periodic
Evaluation Record Community Form. Still, there are some problems
with Armsby's research. Most glaring was his failure to conceptualize
clearly what treatment strategy the crisis team used. Because they
called themselves a crisis team does not mean they practice crisis
intervention. Without this conceptualization of crisis practice, it
is difficult to say what helped the families.

With the exception of Armsby, most of the other authors (Deeths,
1970; Hart, 1971; Riscalla, 1970; Villeponteaux, 1970) who evaluated
crisis practice with adolescents were less convincing than Baldwin
(1968) or Berlin (1970). For instance, the crisis treatment concept-

ualized by Riscalla (1971) and Villeponteaux (1970) is so sketchy that it cannot be determined if they are practicing crisis intervention. In fact, it seems that their treatment approach for adolescent offenders is more compatible with Glasser's (1965) concepts of reality therapy. In their articles, Deeths (1970) and Hart (1970) also present brief conceptualizations of crisis practice that sound more like psychoanalytic treatment than crisis intervention.

In conclusion, the literature reflected limited empirical evidence of the effectiveness of crisis intervention with children and adolescents. This results from the failure of crisis theorists, with a few selected exceptions already noted, to conceptualize clearly the nature of crisis practice. Without clear conceptualizations of practice, a paucity of good empirical findings will likely continue to exist.

Services Related to Theory

In the writer's judgment, the main problem impeding the future development of crisis intervention theory and practice is the lack of clear treatment models. This review of crisis practice with children and adolescents shows that most practitioners are still vague, at least in their writings, in defining and describing crisis treatment. Those clinicians (Baldwin, 1968; Berlin, 1970) who have taken the time to conceptualize their practice concepts have completed relatively successful studies of crisis intervention. But why have so many failed?

It is believed that many have failed because they have not incorporated into practice the writing and research findings of earlier theorists. For example, even the pioneering work of Lindemann

(1944) gave a great deal of information about crisis treatment, particularly the treatment strategy of completing certain psychological tasks in resolving the crisis of bereavement. It was also Lindemann who emphasized that the most crucial part of the client-worker relationship was sharing the grief work with the client. Then, the later works of Caplan (1964), Rapoport (1970), Parad (1970), and Aguilera (1970b) further clarified the nature of crisis practice. Apparently, those practitioners who are still struggling with a beginning conceptualization of crisis intervention are not familiar with these earlier developments in crisis practice.

Conclusion

In summary, most of the crisis practitioners reviewed in this chapter present sketchy conceptualizations of crisis practice. Without clear conceptualizations of crisis practice, it is difficult to even begin evaluating the effect of their crisis work with children and adolescents. The next chapter deals with crisis practice in community mental health services.

CHAPTER X

COMMUNITY MENTAL HEALTH SERVICES

Introduction

The articles reviewed on crisis practice in community mental
health centers seemed to focus on three main areas. First, a number
of authors (Clarke, 1971; Gebbie, 1968; Hiatt, 1970; Morley and Brown,
1969; Paul, 1966b, Polak, 1967) describe certain crisis-oriented clinics
such as the Benjamin Rush Center in Los Angeles or the nation-wide
services offered by the Travelers Aid Society. Second, the focus of
another group of authors (Allgeyer, 1970; Brown, 1971; Fox and Scherl,
1972; Peck, 1966) was on more specific techniques that mental health
centers can use in working with the crisis reactions that often accom-
pany rape or drug abuse. In addition, a number of other authors (Brown,
1969; Gottschalk, et. al., 1967; Oetting, et. al., 1969) have discussed
related aspects of crisis practice in mental health programs. For
example, Oetting, Cole, and Adams (1969) discuss some of the problems
they encountered as community mental health consultants when they tried
to evaluate a workshop on crisis intervention directed to ministers in
Wyoming.

Services Given

A group of authors (Gebbie, 1968; Morley and Brown, 1969;

Jacobsen, 1965a; Paul, 1966b; Strickler, 1965; Walton, et. al., 1971)
discuss the crisis services offered by the Benjamin Rush Center for
Problems of Living in Los Angeles. According to Jacobsen (1965a),
Paul (1966b), and Strickler (1965), the Benjamin Rush Center is a
community-based, walk-in center for individuals and families suffering
from various intensities of psychological stress. The center's 24-hour
walk-in service is available to anyone over $17\frac{1}{2}$ years of age who lives
in the encatchment area. Treatment, in the words of Jacobsen (1965a),
"focuses on the immediate problem or crisis, rather than on long-standing
pathology or on well established character patterns [p. 210]". The
crisis services are brief, usually lasting no longer than six one-hour
visits spread over six weeks or more.

Clarke (1971) in his article entitled "An Analysis of Crisis
Management by Mental Welfare Officers" discusses the emergency services
of a mental health department in a London borough. Serving an encatchment population of about 210,000, this mental health department also
maintains a 24-hour emergency service. Unlike the Benjamin Rush Center,
emergency callers at the London clinic are first contacted by phone
after their initial phone inquiry. When the mental health officer
returns their call, he decides at that time whether or not to deal
with the situation as a crisis. In comparison, Hiatt's (1970) discussion
of Travelers Aid does not present as clear a conceptualization of crisis
service, although he does deal with some important ideas of crisis
treatment with people caught in "crisis-flight".

Polak (1967), in contrast, discusses the crisis of emergency
psychiatric hospitalization at the Fort Logan Mental Health Center.

As part of their emergency hospitalization procedures, each patient, when referred for admission, is requested to come with at least one member of his family to the next admission-assessment meeting. In this way, the crisis team in charge of emergency admissions is better able to evaluate the seriousness of the crisis. In Karp and Karls (1966) article on "Combining Crisis Therapy and Mental Health Consultation", the authors describe how they use their crisis treatment program which consists of mental health consultation to other agencies and professional workers in the County of Santa Barbara, California.

In discussing the use of specific crisis techniques, Allgeyer (1970), Morley and Brown (1969), and Strickler and Allgeyer (1967) discuss the crisis group and its use at the Benjamin Rush Center. In particular, the crisis group is designed to meet the needs of persons ordinarily under-represented in mental health facilities, i.e. families with incomes less than $4,000, Negroes, Mexican-Americans, and blue-collar workers. Brown (1971) and Fox and Scherl (1972), in comparison, discuss the specific crisis needs of drug abusers and victims of rape.

Nature of Services

According to Gebbie (1968, pp. 328-329), the crisis services offered at the Benjamin Rush Center have two primary objectives: (1) reduction of the impact of the hazardous event in the individual and (2) utilization of the situation to strengthen the coping abilities which may help in mastering future crises. In order to do this, the customary procedure at the Center is to see a client for a maximum of six visits spread over a period of six to eight weeks. In conceptual-

izing the nature of these crisis services, Gebbie (1968, pp. 329-332)
discusses four phases of treatment: (1) assessment, (2) planning,
(3) intervention, and (4) termination. Under the assessment stage of
treatment, the worker evaluates the person's ability to function without being hospitalized, identifies the significant people involved in
the crisis, identifies specifically the hazards that are threatening
the client, and reaches some diagnostic impression of the client.
After this assessment is completed, Gebbie believes the worker should
move into the planning stage of treatment, bearing in mind the strengths
and limitations of the client.

In the writer's judgment, this brief outline covers most of the
important areas that should be part of the initial and assessment stages
of crisis practice. However, some question might be raised concerning
the sequence of steps involved in the initial and assessment stages of
treatment. To begin with, the first phase of the initial stage of
treatment according to most theorists should be the identification of
the precipitating event that led to the crisis and the significant
people involved in the problem. Then the worker should explore the
client's feelings around the crisis to determine if he can be helped
as an outpatient. If his crisis reaction is too severe and might lead
to suicide and/or homicide, emergency hospitalization may be required.

According to Gebbie (1968, pp. 330-332), the planning phase of
treatment focuses on determining with the client what can be done to
resolve the crisis successfully. Usually this is accomplished by
agreeing on certain tasks which the client can concentrate his attention.
The next stage of intervention deals with helping the client accomplish
these crisis tasks through the use of such varied techniques as role-

playing, reflection, mobilization of community resources, and whatever
else is needed.

In Gebbie's opinion (1968, p. 329), the resolution of the crisis
indicates the time for termination of the client-worker-relationship.
In her words, this termination phase includes a review of the crisis
situation and how it was handled, realistic planning for the future,
anticipatory exploration of possible future crises and how they might
be met, and planning for referral to other agencies for additional
services or for long-term treatment. This reference to anticipatory
exploration of future crises and their resolution appears to be an
important point. Basically, this is the task of discussing with the
client how the coping skills he learned during this crisis situation
can help him in the event similar life crises occur.

An assessment of articles by other authors (Jacobsen, 1965a;
Paul, 1966b; Strickler, 1965) who describe the Benjamin Rush Center
revealed repetition of many of the same points made by Gebbie. For
example, Jacobsen (1965a) emphasizes that treatment at the center focuses
on the immediate crisis and its successful resolution. In order to do
this, "the therapist strives to facilitate for the patient both more
effective problem-solving and recognition and expression of the often
painful emotions related to the crisis [p. 210]". Strickler (1965)
emphasizes this point by saying that the "primary goal is treatment
of the crisis situation rather than evaluation or referral [p. 150]".

In comparison with the articles written by Gebbie, Jacobsen,
Paul, and Strickler, Clarke (1971) and Hiatt (1970) are much less
precise in conceptualizing crisis intervention practice. For instance,

Clarke deals with the assessment procedures followed by mental health officers in a London clinic before authorizing emergency psychiatric hospitalization. Hiatt, on the other hand, describes a particular form of crisis that Travelers Aid is dealing with — the crisis of flight failure. This crisis category was developed by agency caseworkers who observed that for some clients the interruption of a continued travel was a more serious crisis than the unresolved one from which they were fleeing. Still, in treating this type of crisis, Hiatt, like Clarke, presents only a sketchy conceptualization of crisis practice.

Polak (1967, pp. 151-154), like Gebbie (1968), presents a rather complete conceptualization of crisis practice that deals with the crisis of emergency psychiatric hospitalization at the Fort Logan Mental Health Center. For example, when a patient is referred for admission, he is requested to come with at least one member of his family to the next admission-assessment meeting. During the initial stage of the next meeting, a psychiatrist holds a 15-minute discussion with the prospective patient and the members of his family. It is during this initial meeting that the psychiatrist presents to the family the proposed group assessment meetings that are designed to determine what can be done for the prospective patient. If the family does not object to meeting as a group, they are brought into the larger admission-assessment meeting where they talk with a social worker, two nurses from the ward to which the patient might be admitted, and the team psychiatrist.

In the larger admission-assessment group, discussion immediately centers on what brought the patient to the hospital. In other words, the crisis team tries to identify with the patient and each member of his family what precipitated the crisis and how they feel about the situation. Polak (1967) feels it is particularly important to assess the feelings of other family members because they are often crucial parts of the crisis:

> Our observations and clinical experience with these patients and their families suggest that our patients were admitted to the psychiatric hospital, not primarily because they had the signs and symptoms of psychiatric illness, but usually because their behavior could no longer be tolerated by the people with whom they lived [p. 151].

The assessment made during this group meeting centers around three areas: (1) individual assessment, (2) family assessment, and (3) community assessment. In assessing the individual, the crisis team attempts to evaluate what precipitated the stress, why he has not been able to deal with it, and whether or not he can be helped on an outpatient basis. The family assessment explores family roles and communication patterns with a particular emphasis on why the family can no longer tolerate the patient's behavior. Finally, community assessment refers to the social resources available to the individual and family that can be used in resolving the crisis.

From this assessment phase, treatment strategies usually include one of the following: (1) intervention with the patient, (2) intervention with the patient and his family, and (3) community intervention. The more likely intervention is usually with the patient and his family. Through a series of four to eight meetings, the family unit and at least two hospital staff help the family deal with the processes which led to the patient's exclusion from the group. This is accomplished by focusing on specific crisis tasks like facilitating better communication within the family group.

A group crisis approach similar to the one discussed by Polak has also been used by Morley and Brown (1969) and Strickler and Allgeyer (1967) at the Benjamin Rush Clinic. These crisis groups were begun to provide additional services to specific target groups such as Blacks, Mexican-Americans, and individuals with less than $4,000 annual income. The initial phase of these crisis groups, according to Morley and Brown (1969, pp. 30-31), begins during the intake interview. At this time, the worker assesses the appropriateness of group treatment. If the client wants to be part of a group experience, he is transferred to an open-ended crisis group unless any of the following exists: (1) a serious suicidal or homicidal risk which might not be satisfactorily controlled in the group, (2) psychotic process so severe that it might be disruptive to the group, and (3) non-English speaking clients. If any of these situations occur, the client is then seen individually.

Before the client enters the group, the worker spends the bulk of the intake interview assessing the hazard that precipitated the crisis. In addition, the worker explores with the client his previous and potential coping mechanisms so he can gain a better understanding of the crisis. After this is completed, the worker prepares the client for the group experience that follows. Usually this is accomplished by telling the client that the group will help him in dealing more effectively with his crisis by offering their support and suggestions.

The treatment phase of the group begins when the client enters the open-ended group and is asked to tell why he is there. The worker

helps the client do this by asking him to explain why the crisis has
occurred and why he has been unable to deal effectively with it.
Having completed this task, the group helps the new member clarify
his crisis and the feelings that surround it. Then they give their
support in aiding the individual's attempts to cope with the crisis
more effectively. In this manner, the group, guided by the worker,
helps each member resolve his personal crisis.

Strickler and Allgeyer (1967, pp. 30-31) feel the crisis group
is important for two reasons. First, the group members can support
and even aid the individual in resolving his crisis. For example, some
of the group members may have successfully resolved a similar crisis
earlier. They, in turn, can share with the new group member some of
the solutions they implemented in resolving their own crisis. Second,
the group can be an invaluable tool in reinforcing and sustaining the
client's confidence in his new ways of coping. This support and
sustainment is especially important as the individual begins to move
out of the group.

In concluding this section, reference is made to Fox and Scherl's
(1972, pp. 37-40) article on "Crisis Intervention with Victims of Rape".
In this publication, Fox and Scherl discuss certain psychological tasks
that rape victims must accomplish if they are to resolve this particular
crisis successfully. For example, they believe that during the initial
phase of treatment the victim must be encouraged to talk about the
assault. More specifically, the victim must deal with the following
issues: (1) medical attention, (2) legal matters and police contacts,
(3) notification of family or friends, (4) current practical problems,

(5) clarification of factual information, (6) emotional responses, and (7) psychiatric information. Fox and Scherl then discuss each of these tasks and why they are important.

In phase three or the final stage of treatment, two central issues must be worked through with the victim: (1) her feelings about herself and (2) her feelings about the assailant. For instance, the victim may still feel guilty, unclean, or damaged and she must deal openly with these feelings if she is to resolve the final stage of treatment.

In conclusion, the writer feels these publications on crisis intervention in community mental health services point out a number of important concepts. To begin with, the initial phase of each treatment strategy centers around two issues: (1) identifying the precipitating factor that led to the crisis and (2) then exploring the client's feelings around this crisis. This is followed by a brief assessment period where the worker identifies the client's current coping mechanisms and why they are ineffective in resolving the crisis. Then specific treatment strategies are implemented by the worker. Usually these treatment strategies involve the completion of specific tasks that the client can follow in resolving the crisis. And finally, termination is accomplished as the client completes these psychological tasks, usually within six to eight weeks.

Service Evaluation

On the whole, the empirical research done on crisis intervention with community mental health services is better than the research completed on children and adolescents. For example, in Allgeyer's (1970) research on the crisis group, he presents an extensive case study of six women to verify the effectiveness of group crisis intervention. In particular, this case study shows how Miss A was helped over the crisis of an unplanned pregnancy by other group members who offered their support and suggestions. Miss A finally resolved this personal crisis by keeping the baby and planning for his postnatal care while she continued in a government training program. In the writer's judgment, this case study documents the effectiveness of group crisis intervention with Miss A because it takes her through the entire treatment process which corresponds with the theoretical model presented by the authors. Thus, the authors were able to show that they followed their conceptual framework of group crisis practice.

Strickler and Allgeyer (1967) followed a similar format in evaluating the effectiveness of their group crisis treatment program. For instance, they describe the growth of 30 patients over a six-month test period. At the end of this research period, both authors felt 25 of the 30 patients had showed some improvement with two-thirds of the 25 showing maximum improvement. This, however, brings up an obvious weakness of the Allgeyer (1970) and Strickler and Allgeyer (1967) research. Both studies rely exclusively on the observed evaluations of the therapists who were working with the crisis group thereby interjecting possible worker bias. The reader will recall that this same problem limited the validity of crisis intervention outcome studies with children and adolescents.

This emphasis on case studies as a tool of evaluation is also followed by Fox and Scherl (1972) in their publication on crisis intervention with rape victims. Basically, their empirical research focuses on 13 rape victims who were helped on a time-limited crisis treatment plan. In the writer's judgment, this research is particularly helpful because these 13 rape victims are followed through the completion of certain psychological tasks associated with the resolution of their crises.

Especially disappointing is the research conducted by Gebbie (1968), Jacobsen (1965a), Paul (1966b), and Polak (1967). None of these authors presents any empirical evidence to support the effectivess of crisis intervention. This is most unfortunate because Gebbie and Polak present the most complete conceptualizations of crisis practice of the authors reviewed in this chapter. To be sure, both authors use brief case studies to illustrate their crisis treatment; but these case studies are too brief to illuminate adequately crisis practice. Even so, the authors do present some descriptive data that verify part of what they are claiming. For instance, Gebbie (1968) did a follow-up study of those cases who terminated without the agreement of the worker. He found that three of the seven clients terminated early because they reached a stability in their crises before the sixth interview and did not feel they needed the worker's assistance any longer. By contrast, two of the seven clients felt other resources not identified by the worker would be more valuable in resolving the crisis. Polak (1967), on the other hand, found that 90 per cent of a total sample of 104 consecutive male patients requesting admission at the Fort Logan Mental Health Center had a presenting crisis that precipitated the admission request. In 60 per cent of these crisis situations, the crisis focused on the family's unwillingness or inability to tolerate with the client's behavior any longer.

In the writer's opinion, these findings are important for two reasons. First of all, they reinforce the concept that a crisis is time-limited with some type of equilibrium established within six to eight weeks. In addition, they seem to point out that a client in crisis is desperate when seeking help and if the worker cannot supply it he goes elsewhere for assistance. Second, these findings reflect the impact a family unit can have on a crisis. For instance, in Polak's (1967) findings the family seemed to have an important role in determining what is a crisis. More will be said about this in the following chapter on marital and family crises.

In summary, the empirical research on crisis practice in community mental health services presents a new dilemma. In the previous chapter on "Children and Adolescents", the main failure noted was in presenting a conceptual framework of crisis practice to verify the empirical findings of crisis intervention. In the studies reviewed in this chapter, the opposite problem seems to be reflected. For instance, Gebbie (1968) and Polak (1967) both presented clear conceptualizations of crisis practice. Yet neither author presented any empirical research to support their treatment claims.

Services Related to Theory

In the writer's judgment, most of the authors who describe crisis practice in community mental health services present treatment strategies that are based on accepted principles of crisis intervention. For example, many of these theorists (Allgeyer, 1970; Brown, 1971; Fox and Scherl, 1972; Gebbie, 1968; Polak, 1967) stress that the initial phase of crisis treatment needs to focus on the precipitating event that led to the crisis and how the client feels about the situation. In addition, most of the authors also recommended that a sense of calmness and helpfulness be conveyed to the client in this initial contact so he can feel there is a good chance of resolving his crisis successfully. These concepts are obviously influenced by the earlier works of Lindemann (1944) and Caplan (1964), especially the idea of concentrating treatment on the presenting crisis.

In addition, most of these theorists stress the importance of the assessment phase of treatment in evaluating why the client's traditional coping mechanisms have been ineffective in meeting the crisis. Some of these authors (Allgeyer, 1970; Morley and Brown, 1969; Strickler and Allgeyer, 1967) believe it is also important to share this assessment with the client so he will have a better idea of what is happening and why. The writer too regards this as crucial because the client is helped to deal immediately with his feelings of helplessness by gaining a better understanding of what is happening.

However, none of the authors is very clear in distinguishing the initial phase from the assessment phase. Most crisis theorists (Parad, 1970; Rapoport, 1970) believe the initial phase flows into the assessment stage as the worker and client start identifying the precipitating event. Consequently, it is difficult to arbitrarily separate these two phases of treatment. Instead, the assessment phase is best seen

as a continuation of the initial phase of treatment that continues
to focus on the presenting crisis.

In selecting treatment strategies, most crisis theorists suggest
enhancing the coping skills of the client. However, none of the crisis
theorists and practitioners reviewed in this chapter identify or discuss
those coping skills. In addition, none of the treatment strategies
deal very extensively with termination. Those (Gebbie, 1968; Paul,
1966b; Strickler and Allgeyer, 1970) who do discuss termination usually
identify the completion of specific tasks as the end of treatment.

In conclusion, one of the major problems linked with the work of the
theorists reviewed in this chapter is their failure to test and verify with
empirical research the success or failure of crisis practice. Most
of the authors present conceptual frameworks that are clear enough
to be subjected to evaluative research but for whatever reason the
research is not conducted. This lack of empirical validation, then,
remains one of the main stumbling blocks in the path of crisis theory
and practice.

Conclusion

In the first chapter of this section, it was stated that crisis
theorists working with children and adolescents have failed to conceptualize crisis intervention practice. In this chapter on community
mental health services, the crisis practitioners have failed to evaluate
their conceptual frameworks of crisis intervention. The following
discussion of crisis intervention with families presents probably
the most complete conceptualization and validation of crisis practice.

CHAPTER XI

FAMILIES

Introduction

The literature on crisis intervention with families centers
around four subject areas. First of all, there are a number of authors
(Argles and Mackenzie, 1970; Duckworth, 1967; Langsley, 1968a; Langsley
and Kaplan, 1968; Shields, 1969) who discuss the practice of crisis
intervention in family counseling centers. Other authors (Caplan, 1960;
Caplan, et. al., 1965; Dyer, 1963; Koos, 1950) describe family crisis
intervention with specific problems such as premature births, parenthood, and unwed motherhood. A third group of crisis intervention
theorists (Klein and Lindemann, 1961; Lindemann, 1956; Parad and Caplan,
1960) present generic conceptual frameworks for studying and helping
families in crisis. A final series of crisis authors (Eisler and Hersen,
1973; Richman and Davidoff, 1971) present two novel approaches to crisis
intervention with families: behavioral therapy and interaction testing.
With these four categories serving as a guide, some of the services
outlined in these treatment models will be described in detail.

Services Given

Probably the best description of crisis intervention with
families is presented by Langsley (1968b, 1969) and Kaplan (1968).

Their articles discuss in detail family crisis intervention at the
Family Treatment Unit of the Colorado Psychiatric Hospital. In brief,
the Family Treatment Unit was established to test whether family crisis
therapy could provide an effective alternative to emergency psychiatric
hospitalization by meeting with a prospective patient and his family
before hospitalization. Unlike other treatment plans, Langsley and
Kaplan encourage all members of the prospective patient's family to
deal with the crisis as a family crisis instead of an individual
problem. Argles and Mackenzie (1970), in contrast, present a model
of family crisis therapy for multi-problem families who have not been
helped by more traditional forms of social welfare services.

In their series of articles, Caplan (1960, 1965) and Rapoport
(1962b) discuss the family crisis experienced by a premature birth and
treatment techniques that can help a family resolve this crisis effectively. More specifically, these authors stress the completion of
certain psychological or behavioral tasks in dealing successfully with
the crisis of prematurity. Of course, this emphasis on specific psychological tasks was emphasized much earlier by Lindemann (1944) in his
research on grief reactions. In addition, there are a number of other
authors (Dyer, 1963; Le Masters, 1957; Signell, 1969) who deal with the
resolution of family crises such as parenthood or unwed motherhood.
An example is Signell's (1969) article wherein he explains how the
family crisis worker can consult with other "professional caregivers"
such as school counselors, religious leaders, etc., in gaining additional community resources and supports for the unwed mother.

Parad and Caplan (1960), in comparison, present practice models

for helping families in crisis that stress three main areas:
(1) family-life style, (2) intermediate problem-solving mechanisms,
and (3) need-response patterns. Along this same line, Klein and
Lindemann (1961) present a model for family crisis therapy that
promotes a community approach so "knowledge of neighborhood patterns,
community resources, and current community concerns that may have
relevance to the specific predicament is added to the planning of the
clinical team [p. 289]".

In conclusion, the articles by Richman and Davidoff (1971)
and Eisler and Hersen (1973) discuss how interaction testing and
behavior modification can be effectively used in conjunction with
family crisis intervention. For instance, Richman and Davidoff explain
how psychological testing gauging a couple's interaction patterns can
be used by the therapist to improve a couple's communication skills.
Eisler and Hersen, in contrast, discuss how modeling, role-playing,
and other techniques of behavior therapy are used successfully in
family crisis therapy.

Nature of Services

Langsley (1968b, 1969) presents perhaps the clearest description
of family crisis therapy of the authors reviewed in this chapter. In
his articles, he discusses in detail family crisis intervention at the
Family Treatment Unit of the Colorado Psychiatric Hospital. Most of
the families treated with this crisis model lived within a hour's
travel of the hospital and originally requested the emergency hospitalization of a family member. Langsley (1968b) believes that if this

emergency hospitalization occurs without helping the family system
first the results are usually negligible as the following statement
emphasizes:

> The removal of an individual from his family
> to a hospital is more likely to complicate than aid
> the situation. It removes one member from a family,
> permits extrusion and scapegoating and avoids the
> family problem which may have precipitated the crisis
> [p. 146].

Therefore, Langsley discourages the emergency hospitalization of family
members and, instead, prefers working with the entire family unit on an
outpatient basis.

In discussing this model of family crisis therapy in more depth,
Langsley (1968b, pp. 22-30) explains that the initial phase of treatment
begins when the prospective patient and his family are seen together.
Usually this initial contact occurs when the prospective patient is
brought to the hospital by his family requesting emergency hospitalization. Since this initial request may occur at any time, one of the
family treatment team members is always on call and available around
the clock seven days a week.

From the time the family treatment team sees the patient and
his family, they continue to stress that the problem involves all the
family members. In fact, as treatment continues and it becomes obvious
that an immediate relative or friend also figures in the crisis, the
treatment team will invite that absent party to attend future treatment
sessions. It is also during this initial phase of treatment that team
members emphasize that they will help the family deal with their crisis
by offering professional crisis services. This declaration of help

coming from a treatment team made up of a skilled psychiatrist, psychologist, social worker, and nurse conveys to the family and the prospective patient that this crisis is not insurmountable. In fact, the
family is told during the initial contact that the goal of the family
treatment team is to help them resolve the specific crisis they are
facing and become better functioning family units.

It is also during this initial family meeting that the treatment
team helps the family focus on the precipitating event that led to the
crisis. Since identifying the precipitating event is also part of the
assessment phase of treatment, Langsley is saying that assessment begins
immediately with the initial family contact. In identifying with the
family the presenting problem, all family members, especially the
prospective patient, are encouraged to share their own impressions
and feelings around what is happening. During this exploration of the
problem, missing details or distortions in the account are often
corrected by other family members. In addition, those missing details
and distortions that remain give the crisis team important tasks to
concentrate on with the family.

After this first contact with the family is completed, a return
interview is usually scheduled the following morning which often keeps
the family intact for the evening and the patient out of the hospital.
Along with this return interview, the family treatment team also tries
to schedule within 24 to 36 hours of the return interview a home visit
with the family. This home visit is used to assess further family
interaction patterns, especially parent-child relations, along with
strengthening the treatment contact between the family and the crisis

team. In summary then, Langsley (1968b) holds that the initial goal
of treatment "is to gain entrance into the family within the first
twenty-four hours, to place responsibility for the patient's symptoms
on the family and to relieve the immediate tension sufficiently to
proceed with work on the family crisis [p. 25]".

The initial treatment strategy used by the crisis team focuses
on reducing the level of tension and upset which almost always surrounds
the family's attempt to hospitalize a member in a mental hospital.
Usually this is accomplished by helping the family to see that the
psychotic symptoms of the prospective patient are often attempts to
communicate with the family and ask for help. However, most of the
treatment focuses on the resolution of specific tasks in helping the
family resolve the crisis. For example, a family crisis may be
precipitated as an adolescent attempts to move toward adulthood or
adult sexual behavior. In order to resolve this crisis, the family
might be asked by the crisis team to work out in a family conference
mutually accepted rules for dating or adolescent privileges that are
appropriate and consistent with the privileges given other adolescents.
Sometimes the family may be reacting to a recent death or illness of
a member by placing inappropriate demands on another member that
influences his troublesome behavior. Such a problem, described by
Parad and Caplan (1960), focuses on a mother's emergency hospitalization
for tuberculosis and how the other family members scapegoated a younger
sister. In resolving this crisis, Parad and Caplan also stress the
family's completion of specific tasks such as expressing together their
fears surrounding the mother's hospitalization and the possibility of

her death.

In the treatment plan presented by Langsley, contact is maintained daily with the family for the first two or three days and then the
frequency of contacts is tapered off. By the third week, the family
is usually seen once or twice a week. This pattern of contacts continues for the remainder of the treatment period which is usually terminated six to eight weeks after the initial request for hospitalization.

Unfortunately, Langsley is less clear about crisis termination
than any other phase of his treatment strategy. He implies that
treatment is ended when the family's equilibrium has been restored.
Usually this occurs after the completion of specific crisis-oriented
tasks. However, Langsley (1968b) does believe that termination can
include referral for additional services. For instance, he cites the
case example of a 17-year old boy who indicated during crisis treatment
that he had been having a great deal of trouble in his relationship
with a girl friend. After crisis treatment was concluded, Langsley
referred the young man for the individual treatment of his sexual
anxieties. Still, the main point that Langsley (1968b, 1969) makes on
termination is that it should include an open-door policy. That is,
the family needs to know that at any time they can request and receive
further help. This seems especially important because the family is
reassured the crisis team in not abandoning them.

Argles and Mackenzie (1970, pp. 188-190) also present a model
of family crisis therapy that is very similar to Langsley. Their family
crisis therapy team functions out of the Children's Department of a
County Social Service System and is composed of a psychiatrist, a case-

worker, and the child care officer. Basically, this crisis team is designed to help multi-problem families in crisis who have been totally resistant to help from the clinic and the community. In the initial phase of working with such families, the crisis team first visits the family in an attempt to assess their readiness to accept help. This initial visit is particularly designed to assess the family's reactions to the team's suggestion of viewing the presenting problem as a family problem.

Part of this initial contact also focuses on how each family member is feeling about their desperate situation. As these feelings are expressed, the team pays close attention to family interaction patterns that develop. While the family expresses these feelings of helplessness and despair, the crisis team invites the family to join them in a time-limited treatment plan that will hopefully resolve the crisis.

When this invitation is accepted, the crisis team and the family begin to identify the precipitating event that led to the present family crisis. In one particular case example, the problem centered on a handicapped mother who was having a difficult time getting her daughter to attend school. Coupled with this truancy problem was the mother's inability to relate meaningfully to either of her two daughters. After this problem was specified, the crisis team and the one-parent family agreed to meet weekly for six to eight sessions and concentrate on improving the relationship skills of each family member.

As this treatment plan was implemented, the crisis team also made an agreement with school authorities that no action would be taken against the mother and her truant daughter during the six to eight week period. This is an excellent example of how a crisis team may use available community resources in dealing with a family crisis. In addition, this case illustrates how a crisis team first moves to relieve the tension of the immediate crisis. In this situation, the mother was in danger of losing her children if they did not start attending school. Instead of permitting this crisis situation to maintain a constant threat to the family, the crisis team and the family made an agreement with the school authorities while they worked on the crisis.

Argle and Mackenzie then show how specific relationship skills such as active listening helped this mother and her daughters to develop a better relationship. As this relationship deepened and the truant daughter realized that it was her choice whether or not to attend school, she began attending more regularly and was going three to four times weekly within six sessions.

After reviewing some of the authors who have written about family crisis therapy, the writer has concluded that Caplan (1960, 1965) and Rapoport (1962b) are especially helpful in explaining how psychological tasks can be an important part of crisis resolution. In their various publications, both authors discuss family crises precipitated by a premature birth and the required tasks to be accomplished in resolving the crisis. For example, Rapoport (1962b, p. 50) divides the crisis of a premature birth into the three following time intervals: (1) when mother and infant are in the hospital after delivery, (2) when mother is at home while the infant remains in the premature nursery, and

(3) when the infant is at home.

During the first phase of treatment when the mother and infant are both in the hospital, the mother is faced with the following psychological tasks:

1. To acknowledge that the infant's life is threatened and that survival in the early postnatal period may be uncertain.

2. To acknowledge a sense of disappointment and even failure at having been unable to carry a baby to full term.

In order to accomplish these psychological tasks, the mother must complete certain problem-solving activities:

1. She must prepare for possible loss of the baby with some anticipatory grief reaction such as sadness or depression.

2. Denial of the real threat or too early an optimism and cheerfulness are considered risks from a mental point of view.

3. Since guilt and self-blame are frequently aroused, the mother must be able to deal actively with such feelings in order to reduce their intensity and possible later negative effects.

This same pattern of specific psychological tasks and problem-solving activities is followed through the other two phases of treatment. The writer mentions these particular authors because they have developed the clearest conceptualization of psychological tasks in crisis treatment. Still, the works of Caplan and Rapoport are strongly influenced by Lindemann's (1944) use of psychological tasks and problem-solving activities in the resolution of bereavement.

Signell (1969), in contrast, describes the role a mental health consultant might take in providing crisis consultation to other service

agencies. In particular, she discusses how she consulted with the
YWCA and other program directors in a joint effort designed to meet
the needs of 18, mostly Black, unwed mothers. In brief, Signell (1969,
p. 308) designed a time-limited crisis approach to meet three goals:
(1) providing schooling, so that the girls would return after delivery,
(2) giving instruction in academic courses such as nutrition, contra-
ception, prenatal care, labor, delivery, and postnatal care, and
(3) breaking into the girls social isolation by providing a group
atmosphere, etc.

Klein and Lindemann (Caplan, 1961) present a conceptual framework of crisis treatment designed for both individuals and families.
This framework appears to have real merit because it points out clearly
the communalities between the two treatment approaches. For instance,
individual and family crisis treatment begin by involving the clients
as quickly as possible in the identification and assessment of the
problem. This immediate concentration on why the client is hurting
helps establish a therapeutic relationship because it gives immediate
assistance to the client. Obviously, this can be extremely helpful
and supportive to an individual or family thrown into chaos and confusion by a sudden crisis event.

As the crisis therapist helps the individual or family assess
the crisis and the intense feelings that often surround it, they also
work together as a team in discussing why the crisis has not yet been
resolved and what can be done in hastening that successful resolution.
Then they decide on specific tasks and problem-solving activities that
will help in crisis resolution. Many times these tasks and problem-

solving activities include the use of other community resources such as hospitals, employment agencies, homemaker services, etc. Klein and Lindemann close by stressing that the worker must leave the individual or family with the assurance that if help is again required they can ask and it will be given. This comforting assurance along with a review of what the client has already accomplished reinforces the client's faith in himself and in the worker.

In conclusion, the writer believes that the authors of family crisis treatment have given the clearest conceptualization of treatment of any of the crisis authors. Consequently, these authors can help all crisis practitioners as they attempt to develop and sharpen their crisis treatment skills.

Service Evaluation

One of the most complete evaluations of family crisis therapy is provided by Langsley (1969, pp. 754-759) in an article entitled "Follow-up Evaluation of Family Crisis Therapy". Briefly, this evaluative study involves a random sample of 186 families seen from 1965 to 1968 at the Family Treatment Unit of the Colorado Psychiatric Hospital. In this study, family crisis treatment consisted of an average of 4.2 office visits, 1.3 home visits, 5.4 telephone calls, 1.2 collateral contacts with social agencies, and lasted for a mean period of 24.2 days from admission to termination.

In assessing the effectiveness of family crisis therapy with other treatment models, Langsley used a control group of 186 randomly selected patients who received more traditional psychiatric treatments

such as individual and group psychotherapy, milieu therapy, and
pharmacotherapy. After his study was completed, Langsley found that
29 per cent of the patients receiving more traditional forms of
psychiatric hospital treatment were readmitted within six months,
while only 13 per cent of the family crisis treatment patients were
hospitalized during the same period. Statistical analysis indicated
the difference was significant demonstrating that family crisis treatment patients have significantly fewer hospital readmissions than other
treated patients. In addition, Langsley used The Social Adjustment
Inventory (SAI) to measure the differences in social functioning
between the two groups. Although the differences between the family
crisis treatment group and other treatment groups did not reach
statistical significance, the family crisis treatment patients generally
had higher social functioning scores. Langsley also found that family
crisis treatment cost one-sixth or less than the cost of traditional
hospital treatment. In fact, the mean patient cost for family crisis
therapy was $200 compared to $1300 for more traditional emergency
psychiatric services. This finding is especially crucial in light of
the need for more effective and less costly methods of emergency
mental health treatment.

In a more abbreviated research study, Rubinstein (1972) also
attempted to assess the effectiveness of family crisis intervention.
Rubinstein's family treatment model focused on a team approach to bring
about the resolution of a patient's crisis without using emergency
hospitalization. Briefly, this family crisis treatment was aimed at
mobilizing a family's coping mechanisms and problem-solving skills in

resolving a current crisis. During the six months from July 1, 1969 to December 31, 1969, the family crisis treatment teams were involved with 27 patients who requested emergency hospitalization at the Eastern Pennsylvania Psychiatric Institute. Of these 27 patients treated on an outpatient basis, only 3 were later readmitted to the hospital. Unfortunately, Rubinstein's evaluation stops at this point and does not provide any other outcome findings or comparisons.

Although Caplan (1960, 1965) and Rapoport (1962b) exclude any extensive empirical validation of their crisis treatment with families of premature infants, they do include rather lengthy case examples of how certain families were helped in completing the psychological tasks and problem-solving activities associated with premature births. Some experts (Fischer, 1973; Sellitiz, et. al., 1959) argue adamantly that thorough case studies can be appropriate measures of treatment outcome. The writer also feels case studies can be appropriate evaluation tools especially when they show the implementation and results of clearly defined treatment strategies. In the writer's judgment, the three case examples given by Rapoport (1962b) represent complete case studies demonstrating the effectiveness of crisis treatment in dealing with crises associated with prematurity.

Other authors also touch on the effectiveness of family crisis treatment although their findings are subject to various research biases because of obvious methodological problems. For instance, Duckworth (1967) describes the crisis treatment used by one caseworker at the West End Family Counseling Service, Ontario, California to determine if the agency's service should include more crisis treatment. During a

24 week project, this caseworker carried 51 family crisis cases and held 176 interviews for a mean of about 3.5 sessions per case. In evaluating treatment outcome, Duckworth reports that 30 of the families, or 60 per cent of the sample, had experienced successful resolution of their crises within six to eight weeks. Yet the author does not explain who assessed the outcome of these cases or what criteria were used. Without this information, the study is open to worker and researcher bias.

On the other hand, some family crisis authors (Dyer, 1963; Koos, 1950; Le Masters, 1957; Robinson, 1969; Signell, 1969) omit any discussion of treatment outcome. This is unfortunate because many of these same authors, especially Dyer and Le Masters, study the course of crisis reactions in families quite completely. But in analyzing these author's publications, it is also clear that most of them present only sketchy conceptualizations of family crisis treatment. In fact, most of the authors seem more intent on studying and describing a family's crisis reaction than helping the family to resolve the problem.

In conclusion, most family crisis intervention authors have done a much better job in conceptualizing crisis treatment and evaluating treatment outcome than any other practice area of crisis intervention. This is especially true of the work done by Langsley (1968b, 1969) and his associates at the Colorado Psychiatric Hospital's Family Treatment Unit.

Services Related to Theory

With respect to the relationship between the conceptual model and the actual practice of family crisis treatment, many of the authors reviewed in this chapter follow carefully their crisis treatment model. In particular, the writer feels that Langsley (1968b, 1969), Caplan (1960, 1965), and Rapoport (1962b) implement sound practice models that demonstrate clearly the initial, assessment, and treatment phases of family crisis therapy. Like many of the authors reviewed in previous chapters, Langsley, Caplan, and Rapoport stress that the initial phase of crisis treatment needs to focus on what has precipitated the crisis and how the family feels about the present situation. Then the initial contact moves further into the assessment stage as the family explores with the worker why the crisis remains unresolved and what they can do together in solving the problem. This, of course, leads to specific treatment strategies that focus on the completion of certain tasks and related problem-solving activities in resolving the crisis.

The family crisis therapists have also explained well the importance of the client-worker-agency relationship in crisis treatment. For instance, most of the authors emphasize that during the initial contact the crisis worker needs to convey to the family his willingness to help them resolve the crisis. Even more important, this willingness needs to be accompanied by calm and confident assurance that help is forthcoming. In fact, this spark of hope that the crisis will be resolved remains an important part of the initial contact, especially for families who are so tense and upset that they feel lost knowing what to do. Again, this statement of help is shared with the family by the worker at termination leaving the family free to return if they need further assistance.

A number of unresolved questions and problems remain in further refining family crisis treatment. To begin with, some family crisis therapists still have sketchy conceptualizations of crisis practice. In the future, they will need to analyze carefully what they are doing in crisis intervention. Second, many of the family crisis theorists are not conducting outcome studies. This is unfortunate because without outcome studies it is difficult to improve crisis practice. Finally, family crisis therapists need to benefit from the advances that have already been made by theorists such as Langsley, Caplan, and Rapoport. At present, many family crisis workers seem ignorant of past findings in their field, especially the works of Langsley and his associates.

Conclusion

More has been written about family crisis practice than any other practice area of crisis intervention with the possible exception of suicide prevention. But even including suicide prevention, the family crisis treatment authors present the clearest conceptualization of crisis intervention. In addition, they have also conducted the best outcome research on crisis treatment. Because of their efforts, crisis intervention practice is quickly becoming a recognized and favored approach with marital and family problems.

CHAPTER XII

HOSPITALS

Introduction

The authors who have written on crisis practice in hospital
settings analyze a variety of crisis situations. For instance, a
number of authors (Decker and Stubblebine, 1972; Kritzer and Pittman,
1968; Langsley, et. al., 1971; Munoz, et. al., 1970) discuss the crisis
of emergency psychiatric hospitalization. In contrast, Aguilera (1971),
Eisendrath (1969), and Oppenheimer (1967) describe crisis intervention
with the patient who is hospitalized with a fatal illness such as cancer
or leukemia. Other authors (Burnside, 1970; Florell, 1971; Freeman and
Zerwekh, 1971; Oberleder, 1970) describe additional hospital crises
experienced by geriatric and orthopedic patients. Finally, Birley and
Brown (1968, 1970) and Kirshner and Kaplan (1970) describe how sudden
life crises can precede the onset of acute schizophrenia or ataxia.

Services Given

In Decker and Stubblebine's (1972) publication on crisis practice
and emergency psychiatric hospitalization, they discuss the crisis
treatment of 225 young adults at San Francisco General Hospital who
voluntarily or involuntarily sought emergency hospitalization. With
very few exceptions, these young adults were treated on an outpatient

basis by an interdisciplinary crisis team. In contrast, Kritzer and
Pittman (1968) describe how overnight care in a general hospital
emergency room was used to avert more serious crisis reactions and to
help the crisis team at the Colorado Psychiatric Hospital extend
crisis intervention to troubled individuals and families. In addition,
other authors (Langsley, et. al., 1971; Munoz, et. al., 1970; Raphling
and Lion, 1970; Rhine and Mayerson, 1971) analyze similar problems
related to crisis intervention and emergency hospitalization. For
instance, Raphling and Lion (1970) discuss the emergency crisis clinic
at Massachusetts General Hospital wherein are treated all walk-in
patients on a 24-hour basis.

Aguilera (1971), Eisendrath (1969), and Oppenheimer (1967)
describe crisis intervention with patients hospitalized with a fatal
illness. For instance, Eisendrath explores the role of grief and fear
in dying kidney transplant patients. In this study, the author reports
that those patients who died were distinguished either by a sense of
being abandoned during their illness by significant others or by anxiety
approaching panic about their ultimate fate.

In Oberleder's (1970) publication on "Crisis Therapy in Mental
Breakdown of the Aging", he discusses a crisis treatment program at
the Bronx State Hospital in New York City where 12 geriatric patients
received crisis therapy. These 12 patients were randomly selected
from the 1,000 bed mental hospital complex where one-third of all
patients were geriatric cases. Burnside (1970), on the other hand,
presents guidelines for hospital staffs to follow in crisis intervention
with aged hospitalized patients.

In conclusion, Birley and Brown (1968, 1970) present extensive data compiled through a number of London hospitals that indicates acute schizophrenia requiring emergency hospitalization is often the result of clear-cut crises which most commonly occurred in the three week period before the emergency hospitalization. Similar findings by Kirshner and Kaplan (1970) at the Bronx Municipal Hospital Center indicate that ataxia or paralysis of the lower extremities is often influenced by life crises that occur shortly before the paralysis.

Nature of the Services

The writer feels that the practice of crisis intervention in hospital settings remains unclear, especially when compared with family crisis therapy. Yet some of the authors present interesting, although sketchy conceptualizations of crisis practice. For instance, the authors (Decker and Stubblebine, 1972; Kritzer and Pittman, 1968; Langsley, et. al., 1971; Munoz, et. al., 1970; Raphling and Lion, 1970; Rhine and Mayerson, 1971) who describe crisis treatment and emergency psychiatric care do so many times without referring directly to accepted crisis concepts. Decker and Stubblebine (1972), for example, describe an interdisciplinary crisis team made up of a psychiatrist, nurse and social worker who work with young adults admitted to the San Francisco General Hospital for emergency psychiatric care. Basically, their goal is to use all of their "technical and personal resources in all available modalities of care to reestablish independent functioning of the individuals as quickly as possible [p. 726]".

Still, this statement does not tell much about what happens

during the initial, assessment, and treatment phases of crisis intervention. Decker and Stubblebine do say that the initial contact begins
when the patient requests admission. At that time, the crisis team
meets with him to conduct a rapid but comprehensive evaluation of the
problem. However, the nature of this "rapid but comprehensive evaluation" is never clarified. For that matter, the treatment remains vague
except for the declaration that "every effort was made to avoid allowing
a patient in crisis to develop a stable adaptation to 24-hour-a-day
institutional care [p. 726]".

Rhine and Mayerson (1971) clarify some of these issues in their
article entitled "Crisis Hospitalization within a Psychiatric Emergency
Service" which summarizes some of the crisis treatment used at the
Colorado General Hospital. According to the authors, their initial
approach "has been to consider hospitalization as the beginning of
crisis therapy for patients who the evaluating team feels cannot be
treated initially on an outpatient basis [p. 1387]". In other words,
the initial phase of treatment begins with the emergency hospitalization
of the patient. Admission is usually planned for three to seven days
and the subsequent treatment follows these basic principles: (1) limited
goals, with emphasis on "here and now", (2) immediate formulation and
planning, (3) focus on termination from the beginning, (4) involvement
of significant others, (5) flexibility, and (6) team approach. This
focus is further clarified by their following statement:

> Our focus is on the immediate stress: long-
> standing problems are explicitly avoided. Planning
> and clarification of goals is begun even before
> admission and is reviewed daily with the patient
> and the staff [p. 1387].

Oppenheimer (1967, pp. 44-51), in the writer's opinion, presents the clearest conceptualization of crisis practice in hospital settings. In his article, he discusses crisis intervention with the hospitalized cancer patient and his family. Oppenheimer asserts that "the techniques for intervention and change in this crisis situation, as in other crises, are focused on (1) helping the patient or family develop conscious awareness of their problem, (2) assessing quickly and accurately the total situation for the patient and family, and (3) enabling the patient and family to make a new use of their existing ego-adaptive techniques or to develop new and more effective mechanisms [p. 45]".

In discussing the initial phase of treatment, Oppenheimer believes the essential task and problem-solving activity for the cancer patient is to develop a conscious awareness of his problem, especially in the absence of his formal request for assistance. This means that the first contact with the patient focuses on identifying the precipitating event that led to the crisis and exploring the patient's feelings around this crisis situation. Obviously, this initial contact also marks the beginning of the assessment phase because by identifying and exploring the nature of the crisis the worker attempts to evaluate the patient's willingness and ability to accept reality.

More specifically, the assessment phase of treatment with the hospitalized patient requires answers to the following questions: (1) What kinds of stress are operating on the patient, both internally and externally? (2) What adaptive mechanisms are already operating? (3) How is the patient behaving in this crisis and how has he coped with other crises in the past? In addition, the crisis worker must

assess the role relationships that have existed between the patient
and other meaningful individuals. Usually answers to these assessment
questions are learned by the worker as he explores with the cancer
patient the nature of the crisis and what attempts he has already used
in dealing with the problem.

Oppenheimer is not as clear in his discussion of treatment
strategies. For instance, he mentions in treatment that the worker
must help the cancer patient mobilize his coping mechanisms to deal
more realistically with the crisis. Oppenheimer adds more information
by noting that in helping the patient the worker must have concrete
social resources such as financial assistance and homemaker services.
In addition, with terminally ill cancer patients, Oppenheimer stresses
the need to help the patient, his family, and close friends conclude
meaningful relationships. In the writer's opinion, this is the key
to treatment strategies in crisis practice — identifying pertinent
psychological tasks with the client and then incorporating problem-
solving activities that will help the client complete these tasks
thereby resolving the crisis.

The importance of environmental supports in resolving crises
in hospitalized patients is particularly well documented by Eisendrath
(1969) in his article "The Role of Grief and Fear in the Death of
Kidney Transplant Patients". In his research project, Eisendrath
attempts to assess what characteristics, if any, influence whether or
not a patient survives the crisis of a kidney transplant. By examining
the case histories of 11 patients who died following renal transplantation, he reports that 8 of the 11 patients had either suffered a sense

of abandonment by their families during hospitalization or had experienced extreme panic and anxiety bordering on hysteria awaiting the
outcome of the transplantation. None of the surviving renal transplantation patients suffered from these two circumstances to the same
degree as those who died.

Burnside (1970), in contrast, gives some valuable treatment
suggestions in working with geriatric patients experiencing crisis
reactions. Specifically, she designs a crisis intervention guide in
working with geriatric patients based on her personal observations and
notes from a year's crisis work in a 187-bed convalescent hospital.
Recognizing the usefulness of this treatment model, the writer has
duplicated it in its entirety (Burnside, 1970, pp. 18-19):

Guide for Crisis Intervention for Aged Hospitalized Patients

1. Set up the terms of the contract with the patient.

    A. Explain to the staff what you are attempting to do.

    B. Consistency of visits important; length of time with
       patient gauged by the patient's coping ability at
       that time. If patient coping poorly, try to see more
       than once weekly.

II. Meet the patient in surroundings familar to him.
    Environment should be reasonably quiet.

III. If patient does not bring up problem or reason for stress
     immediately, therapist can:

    A. Listen.

    B. Clarify that which you don't understand.

    C. Intervene immediately in hallucinations, delusions,
       and confusion.

    D. Consistently test reality.

E. Offer understanding but do not give false reassurance.

F. Explain what your limits are, exactly what you can or cannot do.

IV. See the patient for as long as he has difficulty in coping; do not foster overdependence on therapist. Indications that patient is coping better:

A. Somatic complaints diminish and other interests or conversation resumes.

B. Patient not as concerned with self and problems; becomes more outgoing.

C. Patient becomes more mobile, and not so room-bound.

D. Behavior more nearly approximates behavior before the stress or crisis.

V. Bringing closure by reassuring the patient that he seems improved and that he has done well.

In concluding this section on crisis intervention in hospital settings, the writer refers to Char and Mc Dermott's (1972) study of crisis treatment with nurses who were experiencing crisis symptoms precipitated by their abortion duties as nurses in two large Hawaiian hospitals. The crisis began shortly after Hawaii became the first state to legalize abortion on March 11, 1970. Two weeks later, the authors were consulted by staff members of two hospitals regarding the acute psychological reactions their nurses were having to their abortion work. In dealing with this crisis situation, Char and Mc Dermott saw the nurses together in two extended group sessions that lasted approximately two hours each. During these group sessions, the crisis team concentrated on three tasks. First, they encouraged all of the nurses to express their feelings around their abortion work. This catharsis demonstrated to the nurses that most of them were struggling with the same negative feelings. The experience also demonstrated that it was permissible for the nurses to have these feelings. Second, through the support and insight of the crisis team, the nurses were helped to see that their abortion patients had problems also and that their compulsive, promiscuous sexual activity was often a symptomatic expression of a troubled person who desperately needed help instead of rejection. Finally, the nurses were helped to accept that the new law, where an abortion is a matter to be decided between a patient and her physician, was a workable solution to the problem of unwanted pregnancy when practiced under the guide of good medicine.

In conclusion, the writer feels that most of the authors reviewed in this chapter have developed limited conceptualizations of crisis practice. Oppenheimer's (1967) description of crisis treatment with the cancer patient is a notable exception.

Service Evaluation

The authors (Decker and Stubblebine, 1972; Kritzer and Pittman, 1968; Langsley, et. al., 1971; Munoz, et. al., 1970; Raphling and Lion, 1970; Rhine and Mayerson, 1971) who discuss crisis treatment and emergency psychiatric hospitalization present some interesting research findings to support their treatment claims. Still, the authors' research claims are subject to question because they present such poorly conceptualized frameworks of crisis practice. Without a clear description of the crisis treatment, it is difficult to attribute any treatment outcome to crisis intervention. With this limitation in mind, some of the more interesting research findings dealing with crisis treatment and emergency psychiatric hospitalization will be presented.

Decker and Stubblebine (1972, pp. 725-728) sought to determine if crisis intervention could reduce long-term psychiatric hospitalization at the San Francisco General Hospital. Consequently, they compared the treatment outcomes of 315 emergency psychiatric patients treated at the hospital in 1964 by traditional forms of treatment such as extended psychotherapy with 225 emergency psychiatric patients treated with time-limited crisis therapy in 1967. In compiling data for their research, Decker and Stubblebine reviewed hospital records, social service records, death registries, and other public records to assess what had happened to these patients after their discharge. These research findings reveal that the traditionally treated patients spent an average of 5.9 days hospitalized while the crisis patients were seen daily on an outpatient basis for 11.5 days. In addition, 60 per cent of the traditionally treated patients spent additional time in hospitals after their release while only 34 per cent of the crisis treated group required further hospitalization. Finally, 6 per cent of the traditionally treated patients had later committed suicide as compared with only 1 per cent of the crisis treated patients. These findings tend to reveal that crisis intervention treatment is a viable alternative to traditional emergency psychiatric care.

Rhine and Mayerson (1971, pp. 1389) conducted a similar study in which they compared the treatment outcome of emergency crisis treatment at the Colorado General Hospital with more traditional forms of emergency hospitalization as offered by the Colorado Psychiatric Hospital. In their research findings, they report that 80 per cent of

the patients receiving inpatient crisis services spent an average of
7.5 days hospitalized compared to an average of 3 2 days for emergency
psychiatric patients hospitalized at the Colorado Psychiatric Hospital.
In addition, of the 100 patients treated with crisis therapy, only 30
per cent required additional hospitalization after their release.

In summary, these research findings tend to support the assumption that crisis intervention can significantly reduce the length of
hospitalization for emergency psychiatric patients while also providing
long-term results that are at least equal to or better than more
traditional forms of emergency psychiatric care.

Another interesting research project on crisis intervention was
conducted by Oberleder (1970). In her research, she discusses a crisis
treatment program at the Bronx Mental Hospital that was designed to
help 12 patients with an average age of 76.4 years diagnosed as chronic
brain syndrome or arterioscerlosis with psychosis move back into the
community. The crisis treatment included weekly group sessions where
the 12 patients and staff members discussed the crisis of hospitalization
and what each patient could do to be discharged. More specifically,
crisis treatment focused on improving the coping and problem-solving
skills of each patient. For instance, one patient who felt alone and
abandoned by his family was helped in reestablishing what family ties
remained. In addition, the patient was helped to establish other
relationships in the community with various senior citizen organizations.
Within a period of three months, all 12 of the patients had been discharged from the hospital. After a six-month follow-up period, 2 of
the women were sharing a 4-room apartment, 2 male patients had returned

home to their families, while the remaining 8 patients were still
living alone and functioning well.

Birley and Brown (1968, 1970), in contrast, studied a series of
123 patients who were admitted to a number of London hospitals and
diagnosed as schizophrenic to assess what had preceded their emergency
hospitalization. They found that 60 per cent of the patients had
experienced a significant life crisis, such as a death or sudden illness,
during the three-week period prior to their emergency hospitalization.
In a later study, Brown and Birley (1970, pp. 207-211) found that a
similar patient group diagnosed as acute schizophrenia had nearly twice
the number of significant life crises prior to their emergency hospitalization as a random sample of the general population. They then concluded their research findings with the following statement:

> We believe that a number of factors must
> contribute and perhaps coincide to produce the
> combinations necessary for an acute schizophrenic
> attack, and that we have demonstrated one of these
> — some sort of crisis or life change [p. 211].

Finally, there is a brief article by Block (1970) wherein he
discusses the use of the drug chlorpromazine in the crisis treatment
of battle fatigued soldiers in Viet Nam. When taken by a disturbed
soldier, the drug induced 24 to 48 hours of sleep treatment. In the
words of Block, the use of chlorpromazine "proved to be an effective
and efficient therapeutic-diagnostic-management tool for the severely
behaviorally-disturbed and uncontrolled patients in an open, crisis-
oriented milieu ward in Vietnam where no other facilities for managing
such patients existed [p. 354]".

In summary, the writer feels the authors reviewed in this chapter present limited conceptualizations of crisis practice in hospital settings. However, many of these same authors also include research findings that are quite informative and tend to indicate that crisis treatment is as effective as other treatment models while significantly reducing the number of days spent in emergency hospitalization.

Services Related to Theory

In the writer's judgment, none of the authors reviewed in this chapter, with the exception of Oppenheimer (1967), present a clear conceptualization of crisis intervention in hospital settings. To be sure, most of the authors stress that crisis practice is a time-limited approach that focuses on the presenting problem and not on long-standing personality dysfunctioning. Still, these same authors say very little about the specifics of crisis treatment. Consequently, the task ahead for these authors remains the clarification of their crisis treatment plans.

Oppenheimer (1967), in contrast, discusses specific crisis treatment. For example, he stresses that during the initial contact the worker and patient must identify the precipitating event that led to the crisis and then explore and assess how the patient is feeling about the crisis. Oppenheimer feels this is particularly important for the hospitalized cancer patient who must come to grips with the seriousness of his illness if more serious psychological problems are to be prevented. In a similar manner, he then develops some of the more important treatment strategies of crisis treatment. Unfortunately, however, Oppenheimer presents little, if any, empirical research other than a brief case example in supporting his treatment claims.

Decker and Stubblebine (1972) and Rhine and Mayerson (1971) present some interesting research findings comparing crisis treatment with more traditional forms of emergency psychiatric care. However, their conceptualizations of crisis treatment are so sketchy that it is unclear if they are really using crisis treatment as opposed to more familiar forms of psychiatric care.

In conclusion, the unresolved problem facing the authors who describe crisis treatment in hospital settings is the further refinement of crisis intervention in both theory and practice. As this is done, more definitive research studies will be possible in determining the effectiveness of crisis practice.

Conclusion

Unfortunately, crisis practice in hospital settings remains as unclear as most other crisis practice areas. This is primarily because crisis theorists and practitioners have failed to conceptualize adequately the nature of their treatment approaches. Until they do, it will continue to be difficult to differentiate sharply crisis intervention from other treatment models.

CHAPTER XIII

SUICIDE PREVENTION AND TELEPHONE HOTLINES

Introduction

In recent years, a great deal of information has been written about suicide prevention and emergency telephone services. Realizing the amount of material published on these two related topics, the writer has attempted to review selectively and analyze the writings of those authors who purportedly apply crisis intervention practice in suicide prevention and telephone hotline services. Consequently, the writer has grouped the majority of publications into four areas. The first group of articles focuses on authors (Berliner, 1970; Farberow, 1970; Heilig, 1965; Litman, 1970; Pretzel, 1970b; Tabacknick and Klugman, 1970) who discuss the services offered by the Los Angeles Suicide Prevention Center, the first suicide prevention facility established in America. In comparison, the second group of authors (Brockopp, 1970a, 1970b, 1970c, 1970d; Juechter, 1971; Mikawa, 1971; Musgrave, 1971; Torop and Torop, 1972; Waltzer and Hankoff, 1965) describe other suicide prevention and telephone hotline services operating throughout the United States. Third, a number of other authors (Lester, 1971c; Murphy, et. al., 1969; Sokolow, 1971; Speer, 1971) deal with specific topics of suicide prevention and emergency telephone service such as who calls a suicide center and how workers can assist on the telephone

a person suffering from a bad trip induced by drugs. Finally, other
authors (Mc Gee, 1965; Noyes, 1970) discuss the world-wide problem of
threats of suicide and how community mental health programs can meet
the increasing need for services through crisis intervention.

Services Given

Farberow (1970), in his article "Ten Years of Suicide Prevention
-- Past and Future", discusses the growth and development of the Los
Angeles Suicide Prevention Center. According to Farberow (1970, p.7),
over 99 per cent of their first contacts with clients is by phone with
only 10 clients out of a monthly caseload of 500 seen for any length
of time. In order to respond to this yearly caseload of 6,000 callers,
the center now has 30 offices, 12 phone lines, and a staff of nearly
100 professionals and volunteers. Most of the service demands are met
by non-professional volunteers under the supervision and consultation
of the professional staff. Services are available to anyone who calls
for help 24-hours-a-day.

According to Heilig and Klugman (1965, pp. 275-276), the Los
Angeles Suicide Prevention Center is organized into three closely
interrelated sections: (1) the clinical section, (2) training and
education, and (3) research and theory. The clinical section serves
as a 24-hour community emergency clinic with no eligibility requirements,
no fees, and no waiting lists. In comparison, the training and education
sections coordinate and implement training programs designed to instruct
new volunteers as well as sharpen the skills of experienced volunteers
and professional staff members. Finally, the research and theory

section investigates why people take their lives, with the goal of increasing the effectiveness of preventive and treatment measures in the future.

Musgrave (1971) describes the telephone hotline service provided by the Los Angeles Children's Hospital. Briefly, this hotline telephone service gives assistance to adolescents overwhelmed by their problems. By dialing Hot Line, "a caller may have a 'tuned in, turned on' adult to listen to him; he may receive information about free clinics, drug counseling, or draft counseling; he may get the address of a crash pad [p. 757]". According to Musgrave, there are approximately 90 Hot Line services throughout the nation.

Mikawa (1971) explains how the University of Nevada in Reno developed a suicide prevention and crisis call center to counter the high rate of suicide in the area. In fact, with a suicide rate of 26.8 per 100,000, Nevada has the highest rate of suicide of any state in the union. To deal with the threat of suicide and other crises, a crisis center staffed primarily by volunteers and open 24-hours-a-day was begun. Today, the center has 34 non-professional volunteers along with 9 professional consultants. From November 1969 to October 1970, this staff handled 1,951 cases of which 57 per cent were crisis calls.

In conclusion, a number of authors including Yasser (1970) also describe the crisis service given for special problems such as a drug induced bad trip. According to Yasser (1970, p. 25), the telephone therapist must engage the client in calm discussion, emphasizing that the experiences he is having stem from the drug and will end when the effect of the drug wears off. Consequently, the telephone worker maintains telephone contact until the caller begins to feel better.

Nature of Services

In discussing the services provided by the Los Angeles Suicide
Prevention Center, Farberow (1970) and Heilig and Klugman (1965)
present brief conceptualizations of suicide prevention. According
to Heilig and Klugman (1965, p. 275), the telephone worker must first
identify with the caller what has precipitated the suicide threat or
attempt and the seriousness of the problem. In assessing the seriousness of the problem, the telephone worker pays particular attention
to the onset of the crisis and what environmental supports the client
has to help him deal with the problem. For instance, an acute onset
of the problem poses higher suicide risks than a chronic crisis. In
addition, if the caller has little or no family or friends the suicide
risks are higher. The suicide risks are also greater if the caller
sounds agitated or confused.

After assessing the seriousness of the caller's problem, the
telephone worker can proceed in one of two directions. If the caller
does not present a serious suicidal threat, the worker can continue
listening to the caller, "permitting him to tell his own story in his
own way, carefully noting pertinent information, particularly the
specific request being made [p. 278]". Unfortunately, Heilig and Klugman
stop there with the discussion of the non-suicidal caller. What does
the worker do to help? In the writer's judgment, the telephone worker
should try to help the non-suicidal caller accomplish his specific
request. For instance, if marital problems have prompted the caller to

seek help the telephone worker could refer him to other community
services where this help could be given.

If the caller presents a more serious suicide threat, the
telephone worker can see the client at the center, usually on the same
day as the call. Again, Heilig and Klugman (1965) are not specific
in describing the worker's intervention with the client. In fact, the
following statement is the most definitive description of suicide
intervention the writer found in Heilig and Klugman's (1965) publication:

> The aim of this interview is to direct attention
> to the stress that produced the crisis. Usually, the
> patient's problems have run together in a hopeless,
> unmanageable way. We help sort out these problems
> and try to focus on the most immediate ones, helping
> the patient to start working on these [p. 281].

In the writer's opinion, most of the authors who write about the
Los Angeles Suicide Prevention Center present sketchy conceptualizations
of crisis intervention and its use in suicide prevention. In fact, most
of the authors make a definite distinction between suicide prevention
and crisis intervention and claim that their program is based more on
suicide prevention. Pretzel (1970b) attempts to make this very distinction in the following statement:

> In the city of Los Angeles, for example,
> the Los Angeles Psychiatric Services provides
> crisis intervention services based on the theories
> of Lindemann and Caplan, just as, in that same
> city, the Los Angeles Suicide Prevention Center
> carries on clinical services, applying the theories
> of the men who direct it [p. 29].

In the writer's judgment, the Los Angeles Suicide Prevention
Center is practicing crisis intervention with the specific social
problem of suicide. By focusing their helping efforts on the precipi-

tating crisis and stressing immediate short-term treatment, the directors of the center continue to use two crucial concepts from crisis
intervention theory and practice.

Fortunately, Brockopp (1970a) in his article "Crisis Theory and
Suicide Prevention" has explained more clearly how clinicians at the
Los Angeles Suicide Prevention Center do incorporate crisis intervention
in their work. In fact, Brockopp begins by saying that "suicide by its
very nature is a crisis situation [p. 38]". Consequently, the crisis
theories of Lindemann and Caplan and other experts need to be an
important part of suicide prevention. For example, Brockopp (1970a,
pp. 38-40) explains that during a crisis that may lead to suicide the
individual is in a state of disequilibrium and tension which can serve
as a catalyst for considerable therapeutic change. Also, crisis
resolution depends on isolating the client's strengths and mobilizing
them in working on the crisis.

After Brockopp lists these and other concepts of crisis theory,
he describes how the Los Angeles Suicide Prevention Center has developed
certain crisis techniques for helping the suicidal person. In fact,
Brockopp (1970a, p. 40) organizes crisis intervention with the suicidal
person into the six following stages of treatment:

1. Developing a relationship with the suicidal individual.
If the helping person does not have a relationship with the suicidal
individual, his initial step is to establish one. Essential in this
relationship is the concept of trust which will be characterized by
the free flow of information from the patient to the therapist. Also
inherent in this relationship is the feeling which the therapist will
transmit to the suicidal patient, that of interest, concern, and a
non-judgmental attitude.

2. Helping the person to identify and specify the basic problem
he has. The suicidal individual is usually confused and disorganized

and has difficulty defining his problem. When the problem is placed into perspective and specified, the patient will often feel relieved.

3. Evaluating the suicidal potential for acting out. This is usually done in conjunction with clarifying the focal problem of the patient. Immediate intervention or hospitalization may be needed. The subsequent action of the therapist would be largely dependent on this evaluation.

4. Assessing the patient's strength and resources. Individuals who are in crisis often feel that they have no resources to draw on and no friends who will help them. In their confusion and disorganization, they often overlook people who will be willing to help. Examining the crisis situation and the significant individuals in the person's life space often results in finding resources that the person had forgotten about and which can be crucial in his recovery.

5. Mobilizing the patient's resources. The therapist's next step is to attempt to mobilize the resources, both within the person and external to him. In general, the patient should be encouraged to do as much as possible for himself, but the therapist must be willing to accept responsibility to assist the patient in this activity.

6. Development of a therapeutic plan. A crisis is a call for action. Plans may include hospitalization, psychotherapy or other alternatives. The patient should be included in making this plan, or he may not be willing to take his role in it and make it succeed.

In the writer's opinion, Brockopp presents one of the clearest conceptualizations of crisis practice of any author although his description of the therapeutic plan is limited. He might improve the treatment plan considerably by incorporating specific psychological tasks and activities that the suicidal client can accomplish in resolving the crisis.

In concluding this section on crisis intervention and suicide prevention, the writer feels that Brockopp has attempted to present an insightful look into suicide prevention. The other authors (Juechter, 1971; Mikawa, 1971; Musgrave, 1971; Torop and Torop, 1972; Waltzer and Hankoff, 1965) present such abbreviated models of suicide prevention and crisis intervention that it is almost impossible to identify their

treatment plans let alone evaluate them. This is lamentable because
suicide remains one of our major social problems. In fact, the World
Health Organization (Prevention of suicide, 1968, pp. 9-10) reports
the suicide has ranked among the first five to ten causes of death in
most European countries as well in North America for many years. Since
suicide is a world-wide problem, the World Health Organization believes
any suicide prevention program should have a fourfold aim in preventing:
(1) fatal outcome of suicidal acts, (2) repetition of suicidal acts,
(3) the first suicide attempt, and (4) the desire to attempt suicide.
In the writer's opinion, most suicide prevention programs are focusing
on these goals although with varying degrees of success.

Service Evaluation

Most of the research on crisis intervention and suicide prevention
focuses on the characteristics of those clients who call for help.
For instance, Mikawa (1971, p. 5) conducted a twelve month study from
November 1969 to October 1970 at the Suicide Prevention Center in Reno
in an attempt to evaluate who calls the center for service. In his
findings, Mikawa reports that during this twelve month period 1,951
clients called the center. Of these 1,951 callers, 57 per cent called
because they were in crisis, 20 per cent because they feared suicide,
and 23 per cent called for general information that was not related to
any crisis situation. In comparison, Torop and Torop (1972, p. 731)
report that during the first six months of operation the Alexandria
Hotline service trained more than 200 volunteers and received more than
13,000 crisis calls. Murphy (1969, p. 314) studied those clients who

called Suicide Prevention, Inc. of St. Louis and found that most people who call the center on their own behalf are psychiatrically ill with two-thirds chronically ill. In fact, 85 per cent of the callers had sought psychiatric help before while 58 per cent had made one or more suicide attempts prior to the call. Many of these same findings are also reflected in the research of Speer (1971) and Sokolow (1971).

Only a few researchers have studied the effectiveness of a suicide prevention program. Litman (1970), for instance, describes the characteristics of patients seen at the Los Angeles Suicide Prevention Center and than attempts to evaluate treatment outcome. Basically, his study focuses on 238 callers who were later seen at the center and helped with short-term crisis therapy. Of these 238 clients, 50 per cent had only one interview at the center while 39 per cent had from two to six appointments. In addition, the remaining 11 per cent of the clients had seven or more appointments at the center. In evaluating the possible effects of crisis treatment, Litman followed up on these clients after service had been terminated for an average of $24\frac{1}{2}$ months. Of the 161 follow-up cases that could be located, Litman reports that 64 per cent had followed the center's recommendations, with 10 per cent taking "unequivocal action". In addition, he attempted to rate the suicide potential of the 161 clients although the criteria for measurement are never presented in the article. Recognizing this research limitation, Litman reports that only 4 per cent of the clients had high suicide potentials while 19 per cent were moderate and 73 per cent were low. Only 4 per cent of the clients had committed suicide at the time of the follow-up study.

Litman's research, however, posts obvious methodological problems. To begin with, he does not describe in any depth the crisis intervention services offered by the Los Angeles Suicide Prevention Center. Without this information, it is most difficult to say that crisis treatment was even being used. Second, he is very vague in defining his outcome criteria, particularly when it comes to explaining what characterizes high, moderate, or low suicide potentials. These research limitations, notwithstanding, Litman is still one of the few authors who attempts to evaluate the effectiveness of crisis treatment. In fact, most of the other authors (Farberow, 1970; Heilig and Klugman, 1965; Mc Gee, 1965; Murphy, et. al., 1969; Pretzel, 1970b; Sokolow, et. al., 1971; Speer, 1971; Tabacknick and Klugman, 1970; Yasser, 1970), who describe suicide prevention programs and telephone hotline services, do not even mention treatment outcome let alone try to assess it.

In summary, crisis intervention and its use in suicide prevention and telephone hotline services remains hazy. In fact, some authors (Farberow, 1970; Pretzel, 1970b) have attempted to separate suicide prevention from crisis intervention while others (Brockopp, 1970a; Heilig and Klugman, 1965) insist that suicide is a crisis best treated by crisis intervention techniques. As long as this controversy continues, the use of crisis intervention in suicide prevention programs will remain unclear.

Services Related to Theory

With the exception of Brockopp (1970a), none of the authors reviewed presents a clear conceptualization of crisis practice in suicide prevention. In fact, Brockopp is the only crisis theorist who discusses an initial, assessment, and treatment stage in suicide prevention. This situation probably exists because there have been few attempts to link crisis theory and practice with suicide prevention programs.

Yet in the writer's opinion, the suicide prevention services that are described by Farberow (1970), Heilig and Klugman (1965), and other authors contain such obvious elements of crisis intervention that it is difficult to say they are not basing their services on crisis practice. For example, the previously mentioned authors all stress the importance of helping the client deal effectively with the presenting crisis by mobilizing his strengths and resources. Consequently, the presenting crisis is considered the problem and not some personality disorder that may have existed for years. In addition, the concept of giving immediate help to the crisis client is emphasized along with the client's need to be an important part of his treatment. To the writer, these suicide prevention concepts are crisis concepts that were earlier developed by Lindemann (1944) and Caplan (1964).

Recognizing this obvious link to crisis theory and practice, authors of suicide prevention services and telephone hotline programs need to describe in depth the nature of their service and its relationship to crisis intervention. In this way, they will be expanding the knowledge bases of both crisis intervention and suicide prevention.

Conclusion

Like the other practice areas of crisis intervention, suicide prevention and telephone hotline theorists are generally unclear in

describing the crisis services they offer. Much of this confusion is
the direct result of the arbitrary distinctions some authors have made
between suicide prevention and crisis intervention. In the writer's
judgment, no such distinction should exist because suicide is best
viewed as a specific category of crisis that troubles millions of
people.

CHAPTER XIV

OTHER PRACTICE AREAS

Introduction

In this chapter, the writer has included those crisis authors
who discuss practice areas of crisis intervention other than those
previously reviewed. For example, a number of authors (Bennett, 1970;
Brown, 1971; Confer, 1968; Strunk and Jordan, 1972; Switzer, 1970;
Whitlock, 1970) describe how the minister or pastor can effectively
use crisis intervention principles in helping troubled parishioners.
Johnson (1971) and Pollack (1971) evaluate the use of crisis treatment
in school conflicts. Other authors (Atkinson, 1971; Carpenter, et. al.,
1971; Lundberg, 1970) discuss unusual uses of crisis treatment such
as in Lundberg's (1970) article on "Managerial Behavior in a Crisis".
Finally, a few authors such as Bloom (1965) and Rosenbaum (1944) discuss
particular crisis situations as, for example, wartime separations.

Services Given

In his article "Crisis Intervention Techniques for the Minister",
Switzer (1970) describes how the minister can use crisis intervention
in his ministerial duties. In fact, Switzer believes the minister can
be a key person in crisis treatment as his following statement reflects:
"Few persons are in a more strategic position for intervention in crisis

in terms of visibility, availability, and previously established relationships than the alert and sensitive minister [p. 32]". Consequently, he describes in some depth a treatment plan that most ministers can use in crisis resolution.

In another article, Confer (1968) discusses the crisis services of the Lutheran Social Services of the Central Pennsylvania Synod. Serving a nine county area of more than 490,000 people, the directors of the Lutheran Social Service Clinic began a program entitled "Operation Crisis". Basically, this program is designed to provide effective help to people suffering pain from crisis situations. In setting up the program, the directors developed a two phase approach. Phase I consists of a six day seminar discussing crisis therapy, while Phase II concentrates on a twelve-month period of crisis application by the ministers. Unfortunately, Confer only discusses Phase I of the program in his article.

Pollack (1971) in his article "Crisis and Response in College Students" assesses crises and the subsequent behavioral responses of 188 students enrolled in upper-division psychology courses. In conducting the research, Pollack asked the students to describe a major crisis in their lives and how they resolved it. These written statements were then evaluated by Pollack and classified as to type of crisis and the subsequent behavioral response. Johnson (1971), in contrast, explains how crisis intervention can be used by school officials in resolving student-school conflicts. According to Johnson (1971, p. 84), school officials need to reopen channels of communication between students and administrators before most crises can be resolved successfully.

In conclusion, Brown, Burditt, and Liddell (1965) describe the crisis of relocation by examining what happened to 644 families when they were forced to move by the Boston Redevelopment Authority. In their article, they discuss "how the interventive efforts of the relocation social worker, the public health nurse, and the welfare worker can be combined to utilize the crisis of relocation as an opportunity to help families achieve for themselves a higher level of social functioning [p. 249]".

Nature of Services

Switzer (1970, pp. 33-35), in the writer's judgment, presents the clearest conceptualization of crisis practice of the authors reviewed in this chapter. Basically, he proposes a model of crisis intervention that the minister can use. For example, Switzer believes that the initial stage of crisis treatment begins as the minister and client identify together the precipitating event that led to the crisis. In order to do this, he feels the minister should concentrate on the following questions: Why are you here? Why did you come at this time? In addition, Switzer stresses that during the initial contact the minister needs to communicate warmth, concern, and openness to the client while emphasizing that there is no time to waste in resolving the crisis. Ideally, the initial phase of crisis treatment will also convey to the client that help is on the way and the crisis can be successfully resolved.

During the assessment phase of treatment, the minister explores with the client what coping mechanisms he is using to deal with the

crisis and why they are not working. This is important for two reasons.
First of all, it gives the client a better understanding of what is
happening to him and why. Consequently, a client who feels he is
hopeless in dealing with the crisis begins to develop the idea that he
can have an impact on what is happening to him. Second, by leading
the client to a better understanding of the crisis the client begins
to see the minister as a person who can help. This is especially
important for the client who often presents himself to the minister
as someone beyond hope.

Once the crisis has been identified and the client has expressed
his feelings of frustration and helplessness, the minister explores with
the client how he has dealt with other crisis situations in the past.
Here the focus is on identifying coping mechanisms and problem-solving
skills that the client has used in the past but is not using with the
present crisis. Once these successful coping mechanisms have been
identified, the minister helps the client apply them to the present
crisis situation. Put in the words of Switzer, "the therapist, using
the relationship, reinforces those decisions and actions by the client
which are seen as being most effective, and thus assists the distressed
person in a process of learning methods of coping with his problem
[p. 35]".

Switzer's explanation of treatment strategy, however, leaves
many questions unanswered. For instance, he does not discuss sufficiently
what he means by adequate or inadequate coping mechanisms or how they are
used in crisis resolution. In the writer's opinion, the better treatment
approach is identifying with the client specific psychological tasks and

problem-solving activities that will lead to a successful resolution
of the crisis. Even with these limitations, however, Switzer presents
a fairly clear conceptualization of crisis intervention that most
ministers should find helpful.

Whitlock (1970, pp. 38-39) also presents a crisis model for
ministers. Although it is not as complete as Switzer's, Whitlock does
discuss four different levels of crisis intervention that the minister
can use. The first level is identified as environmental manipulation.
Basically, environmental manipulation is crisis intervention designed
to remove some hazard or to change some situation. For example, helping
a client find employment is one way the minister can use environmental
manipulation in resolving a crisis. Supportive intervention, on the
other hand, is characterized by non-specific forms of intervention.
For instance, non-threatening listening is one way the minister can let
the client know he is willing to help even if that help only involves
listening to a frightened and frustrated client. In contrast, generic
crisis intervention focuses on the resolution of crises by accomplishing
certain psychological tasks and problem-solving activities. Here the
minister becomes familiar with what tasks a client needs to accomplish
for the successful resolution of certain crises like death, prematurity,
emergency hospitalization, etc. Then when a client comes to his office
with one of these crisis situations, the minister has a ready made
treatment plan. In opposition to the generic approach is individual
crisis treatment. Here the minister identifies with the client what
he needs to do to resolve a crisis based on his needs and then helps
the client work towards crisis resolution. In other words, there are

no predetermined tasks that the client must follow but only those tasks
that will meet his individual crisis needs.

Whitlock feels most ministers could use the first three levels
of crisis intervention without much difficulty. However, since the
individual approach of crisis treatment requires a working knowledge
of individual dynamics, he feels it is not an appropriate crisis
treatment for ministers. The writer concurs with Whitlock's decision.

An interesting adaptation of crisis intervention and career
counseling is also presented by Brown (1971) in his article entitled
"Career Counseling as a Form of Pastoral Care". Briefly, Brown describes
the services of the Northeast Career Center which was organized by the
United Presbyterian Church in 1965 to help ministers in crisis. In
Brown's words, "this new 'ministry to ministers' has developed in
recognition of the 'restlessness' among the clergy and the great pain
of ambiguity which permeates the church today [p. 16]". Brown discusses
seven crises that can affect a minister and motivate him to seek help.
Two of these include the crisis of integrity which occurs when a man
realizes that his profession and his inner feelings are incongruous
and the crisis of capacity which occurs when the minister questions his
own professional adequacy.

In helping the minister resolve these and other crises, Brown
presents a counseling program that deals more with career counseling
than crisis resolution. Through the use of questionnaires, interviews,
and personality inventories, the career counselor identifies with the
minister areas where he needs further training and then assists him
in reaching these goals. In presenting this counseling program, Brown

does not refer to crisis intervention in theory or practice. Still, the writer feels his article is important because it shows how career counseling can be used to help resolve certain ministerial crises.

Those authors (Ichikawa, 1965; Johnson, 1971; Pollack, 1971) who discuss crisis practice with college students do not present clear conceptualizations of crisis practice. In fact, none of them discusses crisis practice at all. For example, Pollack (1971, pp. 49-50) asked 188 college students in upper-division psychology courses to describe an important life crisis they had experienced along with how they resolved it. Although his findings do not deal with crisis practice, they do explain how many people deal with stress. In his study, Pollack found that many students in crisis deal with the tension and anxiety by changing the goals or activities that led to the crisis. Still, this information does not offer much insight into how a person can be helped during a crisis.

Other authors (Atkinson, 1971; Carpenter, et. al., 1971; Cath, 1965; Lundberg, 1970; Rosenbaum, 1944; Strumpfer, 1970) reviewed in this chapter also present extremely limited theories of crisis practice. This is unfortunate because without a clear conceptualization of crisis intervention it is most difficult to validate the research findings they are promoting. In their article, Brown, Burditt, and Liddell (1965) bridge some of these problems by presenting a fairly compact look at the crisis of relocating 644 families in the Boston area due to urban renewal programs. In the crisis of relocation, they feel the initial contact of the worker is to help the family see the relocation worker as a helpful person. In fact, they have developed such a compact model that the writer has duplicated their treatment plan:

1. Getting to know the family: Establishing the relocation worker as a helping person — developing trust; learning the neighborhood interrelationships; talking informally with people; getting early but definitive thoughts on relocation.

2. Helping residents face the reality of relocation: Watching the advance of the crane; reading newsletters and newspapers; talking about feelings — "You have to move. You don't want to move when you're upset and angry, do you?"

3. Exploring and handling problems interfering with relocation: What the neighborhood has meant; loss of friends, of Lincoln House (a local community center), of stores; medical problems; social incapacities; poor housekeeping standards; financial difficulties. "Maybe you need to talk some more about these feelings before you start looking at places."

4. Agreement about "safe, sanitary, and decent housing:" Seeing themselves in a nice place; what they can have; what they should have; what they want — "I can help if this is what you want."

5. Considering alternative choices: "Have you thought about an area? Where are your friends? Have you ever been to..?"

6. Finding the "this-is-it" place: "Let's go out together and look at something to give you an idea."

7. Cementing relationships in the new neighborhood: The relocation worker as "handrail" — "Have you found a new store? There's a place I know like Lincoln House [p. 251]".

Brown, Burditt, and Liddell's crisis model for relocation presents an accurate and innovative look at crisis intervention. Although their model is brief and needs further definition, they do present basic crisis concepts such as identifying the precipitating stress, exploring with the client his feelings around the crisis, and working with the client in crisis resolution.

In summary, most of the authors reviewed in this chapter present vague conceptualizations of crisis practice. In fact, few of them even claim to have developed a theory of crisis intervention. Consequently,

it is difficult to assess the initial, assessment, and treatment stages
of their crisis practice models. Likewise, these authors say very
little about the client-worker-agency relationship or when crisis
treatment should be terminated. On the other hand, Switzer (1970) and
Brown, Burditt, and Liddell (1965) present more complete conceptualizations of crisis practice that include some discussion of the initial,
assessment, and treatment phases of practice. Still, considerably more
work needs to be done by even these authors in refining crisis practice,
especially around the implementation of treatment strategies.

Service Evaluation

Only four authors (Brown, et. al., 1965; Ichikawa, 1965; Pollack, 1971;
Rosenbaum, 1944) reviewed in this chapter presented any empirical findings
relating to crisis practice. None of these four authors, however,
presents any conclusive findings to substantiate the effectiveness of
crisis intervention. For example, Brown, Burditt, and Liddell (1965)
discuss the crisis of relocation and explain how a crisis model of
intervention can be helpful in resolving this crisis. Consequently,
they present a fairly complete model of crisis practice and discuss in
some depth the initial, assessment, and treatment strategies of crisis
intervention. Still, there is no attempt by the authors to assess how
effective this crisis model was in relocating 644 individuals and
families in the Boston area. A few brief excerpts from certain case
studies are given to illustrate some crisis techniques such as exploring
alternative coping activities with the family. However, the authors
do not present any empirical evidence in support of their treatment

model. This is most unfortunate because an outcome assessment of the project could have been a meaningful part of their research.

Pollack (1971, pp. 49-50) surveyed 188 students in upper-division psychology courses in order to test the validity of three crisis hypotheses: (1) Crisis levels of frustration will produce behaviors aimed at substitute satisfaction, that is, the individual will change his goals and activities. (2) Crisis levels of conflict will produce anxiety, attempts at leaving the field (escape), and disorganization. (3) Crisis levels of external pressure will produce resistance, defensive strategies, and a wider use of ego defense mechanisms. By asking the students to describe an important life crisis and how they solved it, Pollack hoped to gain empirical validation for these hypotheses. In assessing the students' self-reports, Pollack indicates that hypotheses one and three were substantiated while hypothesis two was not. Although Pollack's findings are subject to possible student bias in describing the crisis situation, they do help to explain how these 188 students dealt with a crisis. In summary, Pollack's findings indicate that crisis tension and frustration in these 188 students was usually resolved by changing goals and activities. In addition, external crisis situations motivate the students to use certain ego defense mechanisms like resistance or denial. Unfortunately, Pollack does not offer any case material in further illustrating these points. Consequently, it is difficult to define what terms such as "external crisis situation" mean.

Rosenbaum (1944) reports on the "Emotional Aspects of Wartime Separations". Although he does not discuss or even mention crisis intervention theory or practice, Rosenbaum does present a lengthy case study that shows how "loss or separation from a loved object, whether this loss or separation be real or fantasied, is of paramount importance in producing these melancholic and discouraged states of mind called depressions [p. 338]". Stated another way, Rosenbaum shows how wartime separation can put a family in a state of crisis. Although recognizing this problem of wartime separations, Rosenbaum does not indicate how the crisis can best be treated.

Finally, Ichikawa (1965) conducted research at the Student Mental Hygiene Clinic at the University of Chicago and reported that 25 per cent of the students sought help because of acute distress related to current life situations. In treating these students, he indicates that the therapist usually helps foster the student's ego adaptive capacity so he can deal more effectively with the current stress. Although this abbreviated treatment plan is similar to some crisis concepts, Ichikawa makes no specific reference to crisis theory or crisis intervention.

In summary, the writer believes that none of these authors has presented sound empirical data. Like most of the other authors reviewed in these chapters on crisis intervention practice, they present vague conceptualizations of practice that it is most difficult to complete valid outcome studies. Without clear models of crisis practice, it will be difficult to assess the effectiveness of crisis intervention.

Services Related to Theory

Throughout this chapter it has been emphasized that most of the authors present vague conceptualizations of crisis practice. Realizing this point, it is most difficult to assess how well their models reflect actual crisis practice. In fact, the only possible answer is that they do not. Until they describe in depth, the initial, assessment, and treatment stages of crisis intervention it will be difficult to evaluate crisis practice. Switzer (1970) and Brown, Burditt, and Liddell (1965) have attempted to clarify their crisis practice models, although what they present is far from a clear conceptual framework.

None of the authors has much to say about the client-worker-agency relationship. Most, in fact, do not even mention the concept. Although Switzer and Brown, Burditt, and Liddell do mention the client-worker-agency relationship, none of them stresses its importance. In the writer's judgment, this is a serious omission because the client needs to see the worker as someone who can help him resolve the crisis. Therefore, the client-worker-agency relationship becomes a pivotal issue in effective crisis resolution.

In summary, the major difficulty of relating crisis theory to practice centers on the crisis authors' failure to conceptualize practice. Until crisis practice is described in depth, authors will continue to struggle with the question of whether or not crisis intervention is effective.

Conclusion

In conclusion, the writer asserts that most crisis authors have presented limited conceptualizations of crisis practice. The writer believes the preceding discussion and evaluation of major crisis intervention practice areas has substantiated that claim. Still, the authors of each practice area have contributed in varying degrees to the further development of crisis intervention. In the writer's judgment, the most complete descriptions of crisis practice have been done with families. This is especially true of Langsley's (1968a, 1968b, 1969) and Kaplan's (1968) work at the Family Treatment Unit of the Colorado Psychiatric Hospital. In discussing their crisis models, both authors present comprehensive descriptions of the initial, assessment, and treatment stages of intervention. The other practice theorists are less precise in conceptualizing crisis treatment. In fact, most of them are so general in their discussions of crisis treatment that it is difficult to verify that they are even practicing crisis intervention. As long as crisis theorists and practitioners fail to conceptualize the various stages of treatment, crisis intervention will remain long on theory and short on practice.

PART IV

TOWARD A MORE GENERAL THEORY OF CRISIS INTERVENTION

CHAPTER XV

CRISIS INTERVENTION AND PLANNED SHORT-TERM TREATMENT

Introduction

The purpose of this chapter is to compare the similarities and
differences between crisis intervention and planned short-term treatment.
In order to do this, the writer has selected Reid and Epstein's (1972)
work on Task-Centered Casework as a representative model of planned
short-term treatment. Reference will also be made to Reid and Shyne's
(1969) earlier book on Brief and Extended Casework where they first
introduced the service pattern that later developed into task-centered
casework. Before comparing the two treatment models, however, planned
short-term treatment will be discussed briefly.

Planned Short-term Treatment

Reid and Shyne's (1969) book on Brief and Extended Casework
reports a pioneering study in planned short-term treatment. In their
book, they describe a four-year field experiment under the auspices of
the Community Service Society of New York designed "to test the relative
effectiveness of contrasting patterns of casework treatment of problems
in family relations [p. 1]". In particular, Reid and Shyne were interested in comparing the relative effectiveness of a brief, time-limited
form of treatment with the more traditional open-ended or continuous
service wherein treatment is often extended for many months.

Unlike continuous service, Reid and Shyne's (1969, pp. 62-82) brief or planned short-term service is conducted under the assumption that treatment will be limited to eight in-person interviews following intake. In contrast, continuous service occasionally lasts longer than eighteen months. In addition, one of the essential features of planned short-term service is the worker's focus on the here and now issues of treatment. By identifying clearly the problem area to be dealt with, the worker and client maintain a steady focus on the specific issue during the eight in-person interviews. Sometimes this problem solution is facilitated by improving communication patterns or by discussing openly disputed role expectations. No matter how treatment is facilitated, the worker focuses his efforts on helping the client solve the specific problem he has identified. Continuous service, in comparison, does not usually focus on specific problems. More often than not, continuous service is less specifically focused as the therapist and client shift from one problem to another.

Probably the most complete description of one form of planned short-term service is presented by Reid and Epstein (1972, pp. 20-40) in Task-Centered Casework. Like Reid and Shyne's model of planned short-term service, the worker in task-centered casework begins by helping the client identify the specific problem he is most anxious to resolve. With few exceptions, this specific behavioral problem becomes the primary target of intervention. After the target problem has been identified, the worker and client agree on certain tasks that the client can accomplish in resolving the target problem. Because these tasks are an important part of the treatment plan, the worker is careful in

helping the client establish tasks that can be accomplished within
the time-limited treatment period that usually lasts from eight to
twelve interviews or less. As treatment continues for these eight
to twelve sessions, the worker's interventions, which can include
exploration, advice-giving, enhancing awareness, encouragement, etc.,
focus on helping the client accomplish the agreed upon tasks. Treatment
is then terminated within eight to twelve interviews or sooner. By
this time, the client will hopefully have completed most, if not all,
of the tasks associated with his problem.

It is recognized that the above is an abbreviated description
of Reid and Epstein's planned short-term treatment model. Hopefully,
this cursory review will give the reader a working knowledge of planned
short-term treatment. In the discussion that follows, the writer will
discuss the problems of living most amenable to planned short-term
treatment and crisis intervention.

Problems of Living

Planned short-term treatment and crisis intervention are used
with similar types of problems. For example, both treatment models
emphasize problems of living that normally functioning human beings
often encounter in their lives. In fact, Reid and Epstein (1972, pp.
41-77) identify seven major problems of living that task-centered
casework is most effective with: (1) interpersonal conflicts,
(2) dissatisfaction in social relations, (3) problems with formal
organizations, (4) difficulties in role performance, (5) problems of
social transition, (6) reactive emotional distress, and (7) inadequate

resources. In addition, Reid and Shyne (1969, pp. 105-110) report
that their planned short-term service plan is most effective with
family relation problems such as parent-child conflicts or role
expectation problems.

By comparison, crisis intervention is most often used when
people are faced with life crises that they cannot usually solve by
themselves. Many theorists claim that these life crises can be
character building experiences that will enhance an individual's
personality development. This is the very point that Erikson (1950,
1956) makes in his discussion of developmental and situational life
crises. Consequently, crisis intervention has been used with a
variety of crisis situations including death, emergency hospitalization,
premature births, and other stressful events.

Crisis intervention and planned short-term treatment are both
designed to help people who are struggling with specific problems
of living that many people experience throughout a life-time. Crisis
intervention and planned short-term treatment do not focus on chronic
personality disorders or mental pathology. Rather, both treatment
models work from the premise that the individual or family have
functioned adequately in the past and at the present time are struggling
with fairly typical problems of living. Therefore, the worker helps
the client increase his problem-solving skills related to the presenting
problem. In addition, the problem areas are defined by the client,
with the worker's assistance, in both models. Consequently, crisis
intervention and planned short-term service propose treatment plans
that enable the client to focus on what he wants to change in his life

as opposed to what the worker feels he should change.

Both treatment models tend to be most effective with specific
types of problems but planned short-term treatment, according to Reid
and Epstein (1972, pp. 80-81), is a more inclusive treatment model than
crisis intervention because it is not restricted to only crisis situations. Whereas planned short-term treatment has broader application
than crisis intervention, the latter is a more appropriate model of
intervention in crisis situations because it is specifically designed
for that purpose.

With respect to choice of interventions, crisis intervention
is the treatment of choice when an individual or family is struggling
with a sudden crisis. Consequently, it is imperative that the worker
be able to identify a crisis reaction so the proper treatment can be
given to the client. In a crisis reaction, the client will usually
be emotionally upset to the extent that his immediate social functioning
will be noticeably impaired. For instance, it may be extremely difficult
for him even to discuss the crisis without prolonged periods of crying.
Lindemann (1944) found this to be especially true in bereavement
reactions. In addition, a person in crisis will usually express how
helpless and lost he feels. In fact, many times he has come to see
the worker because he feels there is no one else to whom he can turn.
Although these are important concepts for the worker to keep in mind,
probably the most important identifying feature of a crisis reaction
is the specific precipitating event that has led to the crisis state.
Usually this precipitating stress has occurred one to two weeks prior
to the request for help, although some clients seek help months after

the crisis provoking event. In most instances, this precipitating
event will be perceived by the client as a hazardous event or a threat
to important life goals. Many stressful events can precipitate a life
crisis although certain object losses such as death or sudden illness
are most common. Identification of the precipitating stress is the
key to crisis intervention. In fact, as was mentioned in Chapter Nine,
Bloom (1963) reports that a panel of expert crisis practitioners could
only agree that a situation actually constituted a crisis when a known
precipitating event could be clearly identified.

Planned short-term treatment, on the other hand, is an appropriate
intervention for dealing with many other problems of living besides
crisis reactions. This means that planned short-term service may be
the treatment of choice in most other problems of living with the
exception of chronic characterological situations such as alcoholism
or prolonged psychotic reactions like schizophrenia. In fact, Reid
and Epstein (1972, p. 201) believe that the task-centered model could
be effectively used in most casework settings. The writer shares this
same confidence in their treatment model.

In Reid and Epstein's (1972, p. 54) judgment, neither treatment
model is appropriate with prolonged characterological problems or
severe mental disorders such as alcoholism, drug abuse, or schizophrenia.
Still, a few authors believe that crisis intervention and planned short-
term treatment might also be effective with these more chronic pathological problems. For example, Oberleder (1970) explains how 12 aged
patients all having diagnoses of chronic brain syndrome or arterioscle-
rosis with psychosis were exposed to an intensive crisis treatment

program that focused on the completion of specific behavioral tasks
in preparing each patient for discharge. Within three months, all
12 of the patients left the mental hospital and either rejoined their
families or set up separate households. In a follow-up study conducted
six-months later, the author reported that all 12 patients were still
functioning in the community. Burnside (1970), in addition, also
describes how a crisis intervention program stressing the completion
of specific behavioral tasks was used by a hospital staff in helping
psychotic geriatric patients. In summary, these findings tend to
support that crisis intervention and planned short-term treatment can
be effective with chronic pathological problems.

Treatment Strategies

In the writer's judgment, authors of planned short-term treatment
and crisis intervention discuss many similar concepts in describing
the initial or study phase of intervention. For example, Reid and
Epstein (1972, p. 21) emphasize that the initial phase of task-centered
casework focuses on helping the client identify the major problem with
which he is struggling. Once the major target problem is identified
with the client, the worker and client further assess the situation,
identifying relevant treatment tasks or strategies that will help
resolve his problem. The focus of treatment then shifts to the actual
work involved in accomplishing the designated tasks.

In comparison, many crisis intervention theorists such as
Aguilera (1970b, p. 16) and Rapoport (1970, pp. 286-292) see the goal
of the initial phase of crisis treatment as to identify with the client

the precipitating event that led to the crisis reaction. Once the precipitating event has been identified, the worker and client explore why the event has resulted in a crisis. Many crisis theorists believe this mutual assessment of the crisis reaction is essential because it helps the client to understand what is happening to him and thus reduces his feeling of helplessness. This is crucial in crisis practice because it assists the client in regaining confidence in his ability to master his problem while at the same time identifying the worker as a helpful person.

In summary, the writer feels proponents of planned short-term treatment and crisis intervention both try to identify during the initial contact why the client is seeking help. Stated another way, both treatment models begin where the client is by encouraging him to identify his own problem. This is the start of a client-worker relationship that focuses on the needs of the client and lets him know that he is important in the treatment process. At the same time, this focus on the presenting problem is an example of directive worker intervention that characterizes both crisis intervention and planned short-term service.

Still, there are a number of important differences between the two models in the initial stage of treatment. To begin with, the initial stage of crisis intervention begins on the assumption that the client is in a state of crisis. Consequently, the worker's treatment efforts focus on helping the client identify and resolve the crisis. In fact, the successful resolution of the client's crisis remains the main goal of treatment. In the initial stage of task-centered casework,

the worker does not begin on the assumption that the client is in a
state of crisis. Rather, the worker views the client as a person who
is struggling with a problem of living that may or may not have existed
for an extended time. Therefore, he may not be as highly motivated
as the crisis client in resolving his problem. This is why the initial
contact in task-centered casework focuses exclusively on problem
identification and specific behavioral tasks that the client can
accomplish in resolving the problem. This point is stressed by Reid
and Epstein (1972) in the following passage:

> But as we know, many of the problems clients
> bring to social agencies are chronic in nature.
> Difficulties in family relations, for example,
> usually fall into this category. While he is
> normally troubled, the client with a long-standing
> problem often does not appear to be in the throes
> of a crisis. In fact, it is often difficult to
> determine what exactly precipitated his decision to
> seek help [p. 81].

In addition, the writer feels the two models of intervention
present different concepts of the client-worker contract. In task-
centered casework, the client-worker contract is one of the more
important points of discussion during the initial phase of treatment.
As part of this contract, the worker and client identify a target
problem that will be the focus of their work together. Once this
target problem is identified, the worker and client then formulate
tasks that define what the client will do in resolving his problem.
Then, the final step of the client-worker contract focuses on the
length of treatment which is usually set at eight to twelve interviews.
If any part of this contract cannot be negotiated with the client, the
worker usually terminates treatment. For example, Reid and Epstein

(1972, p. 65) stress that if motivation is lacking and the client
does not acknowledge a target problem within an exploration period of
two or three interviews the worker should terminate the contact,
according to an understanding reached with the client prior to the
designated period of "problem search".

In the writer's opinion, crisis theorists are still unclear
in their discussion of the client-worker contract. Some theorists
such as Rapoport (1970) and Aguilera (1970b) stress that during the
initial interview it is important that the worker convey a sense of
hope to the client. Usually this sense of hope centers on the worker's
pledge that they will see the crisis through together. Still, none
of the remaining crisis authors identified or even discussed this
pledge as part of the client-worker contract. This is unfortunate
because it appears likely that a mutually accepted contract could
enhance the effectiveness of crisis practice.

Shifting the discussion to the assessment stage of treatment,
crisis intervention and planned short-term theorists both consider
the assessment of the client's problem to be an ongoing process that
begins with the initial contact. Consequently, neither model separates
the assessment stage from the ongoing treatment. This ongoing assessment
in task-centered casework is reflected in the following statement by
Reid and Epstein (1972):

> The model contains no 'diagnostic phase'.
> The practitioner continually makes diagnostic
> judgments which both guide and are guided by his
> activities. These judgments are first concerned
> with classification, specification, and exploration
> of the clients' problems; then with assessment of
> possible client tasks and finally with evaluation
> of his efforts to achieve tasks agreed upon [p. 22].

This assessment of the client's ability to accomplish certain tasks has also been an important part of crisis treatment. In working with mothers of premature infants, Caplan (1960, 1965) and Rapoport (1962b) both emphasize the mother's need to complete certain psychological tasks. In order to do this, the worker needs to assess how he can best help the mother complete these tasks. Unfortunately, neither Caplan or Rapoport discuss how this assessment can best be done.

It also appears that crisis theorists place more emphasis initially on assessing the client's current social functioning although this is also a part of task-centered casework. Yet in the initial crisis contact, the worker is faced with a very specific task that focuses on deciding whether or not the client can be seen on an outpatient basis. This is an important assessment because severe crisis reactions can pose serious suicidal or homicidal risks. Consequently, much of the initial contact is spent exploring with the client his feelings around the crisis. If this exploration reveals a possible suicidal or homicidal risk, the worker often transfers the client to inpatient services or emergency hospitalization care where he will receive more appropriate help.

This initial client assessment is also part of task-centered casework although it is designed to accomplish a different goal. In assessing the client's problem, Reid and Epstein (1972, p. 24) both emphasize that task-centered casework is not designed for chronic pathological problems like alcoholism or schizophrenia. If during the initial contact these types of problems are either identified by the client or inferred from his actions, task-centered casework or any other model of planned short-term treatment should not be used unless the target problem is a problem of living. The same rule holds true for crisis intervention.

It is not difficult to understand why crisis intervention and planned short-term treatment theorists use similar treatment strategies in helping clients resolve their problems. For instance, proponents of each model use a time-limited treatment plan. In crisis treatment, this time-limited treatment approach is especially important since most crisis reactions are resolved for better or for worse in six to eight weeks. In addition, both treatment approaches stress the importance of specific psychological tasks or problem-solving activities in resolving the crisis or problem of living. For instance, Reid and Epstein (1972, pp. 117-118) discuss the case of a twenty-two year old man who applied for help because of his failure in school and work. Identifying his failure in school and work as the target problem, the therapist used specific tasks to help him improve his work performance. One of these tasks helped him to increase his work output by reducing the number of distractions he was experiencing on the job. Similarily, Fox and Scherl (1972) explain how a series of psychological tasks helped 13 rape victims resolve their personal crises.

The writer, however, believes that Reid and Epstein's model of task-centered casework explains much better than any crisis theorist how these treatment strategies are implemented. For instance, Reid and Epstein (1972, pp. 23-24) explain how specific types of communication are used in helping the client resolve his target problem. More specifically, these communication strategies include: (1) exploration of the client's problem, task possibilities, and task-related behavior;

(2) structuring the treatment relationship and communication within it;
(3) enhancing the client's awareness in ways to help him overcome
obstacles to, or otherwise facilitate, task achievement; (4) encouragement of task-directed behavior; and (5) suggesting means of task
accomplishment. In the writer's judgment, these same communication
skills can also be used in helping the client successfully resolve a
crisis.

Crisis intervention and planned short-term treatment also discuss
many similar ideas around the termination of service and the assessment
of treatment outcome. For instance, the writer has already mentioned
that both intervention models focus on time-limited treatment that
usually ends within eight to twelve interviews. In addition, both
models emphasize that the assessment of treatment outcome is primarily
based on how well the client has accomplished specific psychological
or behavioral tasks. However, there are some important differences
between the two treatment approaches. To begin with, the process of
terminating treatment is begun in the initial phase of task-centered
casework when the worker and client contract for eight to twelve
sessions. In the initial phase of crisis treatment, the worker does
not specify the exact number of interviews although he often shares
with the client that most crises are resolved within six to eight weeks.
The treatment focus maintained by the worker, however, is not on this
specific number of interviews. Rather, he lets the client know that
they will be meeting until the crisis is resolved.

In task-centered casework, treatment is terminated in the last
scheduled interview even when the client has not accomplished all of

the tasks relating to his target problem. During the last session,
Reid and Epstein (1972) state "the client is helped to identify his
achievements, apply what he has done to remaining problems, and define
future tasks that he might undertake on his own [p. 23]". Only in
exceptional cases does the worker extended treatment beyond the earlier
agreed-upon limits. In contrast, most crisis theorists believe service
should be terminated only when the crisis has been resolved. However,
in making this statement, none of the practitioners presents clear
guidelines in helping the worker determine when a crisis is resolved.
Many theorists (Caplan, 1965; Fox and Scherl, 1972; Rapoport, 1962b)
imply that a crisis is resolved when certain psychological tasks have
been accomplished although they are far from agreement on this point.

Client-Worker-Agency Relationship

With respect to the client-worker relationship, crisis intervention and planned short-term treatment are extremely client-centered
and focus on helping the client resolve the problems he identifies.
Crisis intervention is designed to help the client resolve a crisis
situation that is temporarily interfering with his social functioning.
Consequently, the initial phase of crisis practice centers on identifying
with the client the precipitating event that led to the crisis. Much
of the initial contact with the worker is spent helping the client
understand why the crisis has occurred so he will not feel so helpless
and lost. In comparison, the worker in task-centered casework helps the
client identify what problem of living he is struggling with. In fact, in
most instances the target problem identified by the client becomes the

focus of treatment.

However, it appears to the writer that task-centered theorists put more initial responsibility on the client for his own treatment than most crisis practitioners. This is particularly true as the worker and client negotiate their treatment contract which states that the client will work on the problems he identifies. In fact, if after two or three sessions the client cannot identify a target problem, the worker does not devise his own. Instead, he usually terminates his contact with the client.

Crisis theorists also acknowledge that their treatment plan requires the active involvement of the client and therefore may provide a growth experience for the client. Most crisis theorists, however, admit that during the initial stages of treatment the client often becomes extremely dependent on the worker. This can be expected because crisis reactions can be so severe that all some clients want initially is for the worker to shield them from the calamity. Consequently, the early stages of crisis treatment often involve doing things for the client that he cannot do for himself. Brandon (1970, p. 631) explains this point well and emphasizes that before movement can begin the worker may have to complete certain tasks for the client. In other words, during the initial stages of crisis treatment the worker may have to meet the client's dependency needs. But as treatment continues, the client takes more responsibility for his own treatment.

In addition, crisis theorists emphasize the growth promoting aspect of treatment more than planned short-term treatment practitioners although Reid and Epstein (1972, p. 23) do discuss the importance of always defining future tasks with the client at the close of treatment. This may be a fine distinction but crisis theorists do seem to stress this future planning more than the authors of task-centered casework. For example, at the conclusion of crisis treatment Aguilera (1970b, pp. 15-17) explains how the worker uses anticipatory guidance in helping the client reinforce his treatment gains. During this final stage of anticipatory guidance, the worker summarizes with the client the adaptive coping mechanisms and skills he has acquired in dealing successfully with the crisis and then explores how these skills will help him in resolving future crisis situations. The worker then concludes this final stage of anticipatory guidance by assuring the client that he can feel free to return anytime for help.

Although throughout this discussion the client-centered characteristics of these two models have been stressed it should also be recognized that the worker often takes a directive role in the client-worker relationship. This may seem contradictory, yet it is a characteristic of both models. For instance, in the early stages of crisis treatment the worker often assumes a directive role by completing certain tasks for the client. As treatment continues, however, the worker puts more responsibility on the client in completing these tasks for himself. By placing this increased responsibility on the client, the worker is still being directive because he is structuring what he will and what he will not do for the client. Reid and Epstein (1972, pp. 176-191) discuss a similar process when they identify how the worker can use specific communication skills to guide the client's actions and better ensure his completion of the treatment tasks.

In discussing the client-worker-agency role, crisis theorists along with task-centered practitioners are less clear about the agency's function than they are about the client-worker relationship. In fact, Reid and Epstein (1972, pp. 200-215) limit their discussion of the agency role to how different social work agencies can incorporate task-centered casework into their treatment programs. Unfortunately, this does not begin to explain an agency's role in task-centered casework. Most of the crisis theorists are also silent in discussing the agency's role in crisis treatment although Parad (1971, p. 201) suggests that any crisis agency should consider the following administrative procedures:

1. The elimination of waiting lists.

2. The avoidance of complex screening so treatment will be simultaneous with diagnosis.

3. The development of an open door policy for those who may require further services when faced with new crisis.

4. The use of a built-in policy of preplanned follow-up interviews to provide feedback about the effectiveness of services.

In the writer's judgment, the above are important aspects of the client-worker-agency relationship in crisis treatment and should be considered seriously by all crisis facilities. In addition, the elimination of waiting lists and the avoidance of complex intake screening would seem worthy of consideration by any planned short-term treatment agency. In fact, the very nature of task-centered casework demands that an agency follow all four of these guidelines.

Relationship to Other Theories

In discussing the relationship of task-centered casework to other theories of human behavior, Reid and Epstein (1972) acknowledge that they have used a number of different theories in constructing their model as the following statement indicates:

> First, most of the theoretical constructs
> and propositions we have developed are either
> drawn from or related to larger bodies of theory
> including general systems theory, communication
> theory, role theory, psychoanalytic theory, and
> certain theories of learning [p. 29].

It appears that task-centered theorists have made particularly good use of communication theory in their treatment model. In fact, Reid and Epstein (1972, pp. 176-191) have devised a communication strategy that helps the worker guide the client in identifying the target problems of treatment while also establishing tasks for the resolution of these problems. In addition, the authors present a comprehensive discussion of how communication skills such as exploration, support, and encouragement can be used in helping the client to accomplish these therapeutic tasks. In the writer's judgment, Reid and Epstein present one of the best examples of how communication strategies can be used in another treatment model.

Reid and Epstein (1972, p. 29) also state that their model contains a number of open areas that the worker can fill with whatever theory or body of knowledge works best. For example, the authors do not present a diagnostic model for the worker to follow although diagnostic judgments are an ongoing part of task-centered casework. Consequently, the worker is left to his own best judgment in adopting

any particular diagnostic scheme to task-centered casework. For some
workers, the developmental model of Erikson (1950, 1956) might be a
useful diagnostic tool. Other practitioners might prefer a diagnostic
model like Hollis' (1964) person-in-the-situation.

In addition, the two task-centered theorists do not present
a theory of personality development in explaining the client's behavior.
Instead, they suggest that the worker use whatever theory of human
behavior he is most comfortable with in helping his clients. The
following statement from Reid and Epstein (1972) explains this idea
well:

> Similarly we offer no theory of personality
> development or functioning to explain the client's
> behavior. Thus let us suppose a client has problems
> concerning her depression over having given birth
> to a mongoloid infant, compounded by conflicts with
> the hospital staff. A practitioner using our model
> to help the client might use psychoanalytic theories
> of maternal reactions to births of defective children,
> crisis theory, theories of depression and organizational
> theory [p. 29].

Crisis theorists have also borrowed many of their concepts and
practice principles from other theories of human behavior and social
intervention. However, most crisis theorists do not acknowledge this
as openly as do Reid and Epstein. In fact, Rapoport (1970) is the only
major theorist who acknowledges that crisis practice is primarily
an eclectic treatment model: "Crisis theory represents a synthesis
of concepts, empirical observations, and clinical insights drawn from
many behavioral and social service areas [p. 271]". Crisis theorists,
however, have used certain treatment models more than others. For
example, much of crisis theory is based on the work of developmental

or ego psychologists such as Hartman (1958) who were instrumental in describing how the human organism copes with a changing environment. In fact, Caplan's crisis concept of homeostasis is borrowed from the writings of Rado (Aguilera, 1970b, p. 2), an early ego psychologist. Yet an even more significant contribution was made by Erikson (1950, 1956) in his extensive study of maturational and situational crises and how they are a part of normal personality development. For instance, Erikson was one of the first personality theorists who believed that developmental crises could be significant periods of personality development and human growth. This growth concept was incorporated into crisis theory by Caplan, Parad, Rapoport, and other leading crisis experts.

Many crisis theorists have also used systems theory as an important part of crisis intervention. For instance, Hill (1949, 1958) and Langsley (1968b, 1969) have used systems theory extensively in treating families in crisis. By acknowledging that the family is a system of interlocking relationships, Hill and Langsley both illustrate how a crisis affects the family system and how the worker can intervene appropriately. Parad (1966) has also developed a systems approach to crisis intervention especially as it relates to community mental health programming.

In summary, crisis theorists and planned short-term practitioners have borrowed many of their concepts and principles from other treatment models. Yet both treatment models have added to these borrowed concepts. Task-centered casework, in particular, has added new knowledge to communication theory and how it is used in time-limited treatment.

On the other hand, crisis theorists have given the practitioner a new synthesis of more familiar treatment concepts and shown how they can be used with most crisis reactions.

Conclusion

In this chapter, the similarities and differences between crisis intervention and planned short-term treatment have been discussed. In many ways, the two models are alike. For example, both treatment plans are client-centered and involve the client in his own treatment. At the same time, the crisis worker and the task-centered practitioner are often directive in guiding the client toward the resolution of his problem. In addition, both treatment models use psychological or behavioral tasks in helping the client deal more effectively with his presenting problem. Task-centered casework, however, is a more inclusive model of social intervention than crisis practice. Consequently, task-centered casework can be adapted to more problems of living. However, when the client is experiencing a crisis reaction, crisis intervention is still the treatment of choice. Finally, it is the writer's judgment that task-centered theorists have presented a much clearer conceptualization of practice than crisis theorists.

CHAPTER XVI

A GENERAL THEORY OF CRISIS INTERVENTION

Introduction

In this chapter, the writer will present a general theory of
crisis intervention designed to be used in most practice settings.
In fact, it is hoped that this general crisis model will benefit all
clinicians wherever they may be employed. In the presentation, an
effort has been made to synthesize much of what has already been said
about crisis theory and practice along with some of the writer's own
ideas and suggestions. The discussion will follow the assessment
framework the writer used earlier in evaluating the different theories
of crisis intervention (see Chapter Two, pages 8-10).

Crisis Conceptualization

Defining a Crisis

The writer believes that Caplan's (1964, pp. 39-40) definition
of a crisis as "an upset of a steady state" is a good beginning
definition. This crisis definition becomes even clearer when the
principle of homeostasis is added. Normally, the human organism
constantly strives to maintain a homeostatic balance with the
outside environment. When this delicate balance is threatened by
either physiological or psychological forces, the human organism

engages in problem-solving activities designed to restore this homeostatic balance. For example, if a young man with a wife and family
of four loses his job he may find himself in a crisis situation. Before
the crisis becomes too great, however, he will often use familiar
problem-solving activities and coping skills in dealing with the situation. Many times he will contact the same friends and relatives he
used earlier in helping him find employment. In addition, he may visit
his university's placement center or call a number of employment agencies
in seeking work. Often a more severe crisis reaction is averted because
he finds employment in using these familiar problem-solving activities
and coping skills. When these familiar patterns of social functioning
do not help the individual solve a problem, a more serious crisis
reaction may follow that leaves the individual feeling hopelessly lost
and confused.

In other words, a crisis exists when an individual is faced with
a problem that seems to have no immediate solution. Many times the
problem seems to have no immediate solution because the individual
cannot resolve the crisis with his normal problem-solving skills.
This is one reason why individuals in crisis often seem so helpless
and disoriented. They believe they have done everything possible to
solve the problem but it still persists. In addition, the problem
has become a crisis because it poses a serious threat to life goals
or is a loss the individual feels he cannot endure. As Parad (1965b,
p. 285) points out so well, the individual's perception of what
constitutes a crisis becomes an important variable in crisis theory.
For example, unemployment may throw one individual and his family into

a state of crisis while another individual may view the situation as
a real opportunity to begin doing what he really wants to accomplish
in life.

In further elaborating on the effects of a crisis, most theorists
stress that it can be a period of important personality growth and
development. This concept, of course, is based on the pioneering work
of Erikson (1950, 1956) and his theory of human development. This is
an important concept for crisis workers to remember. In fact, crisis
intervention is as much a tool of prevention as treatment because it
may help the client to acquire problem-solving skills that he can use
effectively in future crises. This is one reason why Parad (1966)
and other theorists believe that crisis intervention programs should
be an integral part of any community mental health service.

In conclusion, it should be recognized that prior to a crisis
most clients have functioned quite normally. Hence, crisis theory does
not presuppose any chronic pathology in the client although in some
instances this could be true. Consequently, crisis intervention is
designed to return the client to a level of social functioning as high
as or higher than before the crisis.

Crisis Stages

As Caplan (1965) has aptly illustrated, most crisis reactions
follow four distinct phases. The first stage of crisis is the initial
rise in tension that results from the precipitating stress. When this
tension begins to mount, the client will usually try to resolve the
crisis by using familiar problem-solving activities and coping skills.

The second stage of crisis is characterized by increased tension because the client's traditional problem-solving activities and coping skills have not resolved the crisis. During this second stage of crisis, the client often uses emergency problem-solving skills to decrease the tension. As these emergency activities fail to reduce the tension, the client enters the third stage of the crisis reaction. Now the tension has become so great that the client may experience acute depression because he feels helpless and lost. Other clients may become extremely hostile and try to strike back at whatever they feel is causing or contributing to their misery. It is during this third stage of the crisis reaction that the client may pose a serious suicidal or homicidal risk. In the fourth stage of crisis, the client usually follows one of two paths. If tension continues to increase during the fourth stage, the client may experience a major breakdown in his social functioning and mental processes. This is the very point Brown and Birley (1968) develop in their research article entitled "Crisis and Life Changes and the Onset of Schizophrenia". On the other hand, the client may resolve the crisis during this final stage by using maladaptive forms of behavior that decrease tension but further impair his future social functioning. Consequently, the client becomes increasingly more vulnerable to future crises which may result in major emotional and mental disorders such as schizophrenia and depressive psychosis.

In order to best help the crisis client, it is important that the worker extend crisis intervention services before the client enters this final stage. In fact, the client's probable prognosis is much better if he can receive help during the second stage of crisis when his tension level is still manageable. It is during this second stage of crisis that the client is most motivated to seek and accept help. Reuben Hill (1949) found this to be especially true of families in crisis and even developed a pictoral representation of how this happens. Sachs (1968, p. 113) has taken these same concepts and, using Hill's earlier illustration, developed the following model of a crisis reaction:

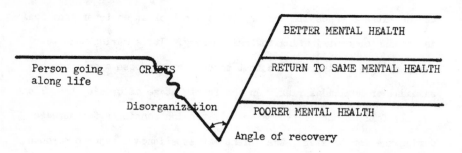

In Sachs' illustration, the reference to "angle of recovery" refers to when the client first seeks help. If the client seeks aid during the second or third stage of the crisis, the chances are good that the worker can help him attain a level of social functioning equal to or better than his pre-crisis state. If the client waits until the final stage of the crisis in seeking help, it will be extremely difficult for him to regain his pre-crisis level of functioning.

Crisis reactions not only follow certain identifiable stages but are also time-limited. Usually most crisis reactions are resolved for better or for worse within six to eight weeks. In other words, a client experiencing a crisis will normally finish all four stages of the crisis reaction within six to eight weeks. Consequently, immediate intervention is needed if the client has any hope of resolving success-fully the crisis and improving his social functioning. This need for immediate help is stressed by most crisis theorists, although Langsley's (1969) family crisis research shows conclusively the effects of immediate crisis treatment.

Different Types of Crisis

Most crisis theorists divide crisis reactions into two categories: maturational or developmental and situational or accidental crises. These crisis classifications have been borrowed from Erikson's (1950, 1956) theory of developmental psychology. The writer believes that Erikson's framework is still appropriate for describing different types of crisis reactions, especially since it includes a discussion of relevant tasks for resolving the crisis.

According to Erikson, maturational or developmental crises are transitional periods in personality development characterized by cognitive and affective upset. Common examples of these types of developmental crises would be infancy, childhood, adolescence, and other stages of normal personality development. Situational or accidental crises, in comparison, are periods of psychological and behavioral upset precipitated by life hazards that usually inflict significant losses on the client. Lindemann's (1944) study of bereave-ment is a classic example of how sudden death can plunge individuals and families into severe situational crises. Other examples of situational crises include emergency hospitalization, unwanted or illegitimate pregnancy, rape, etc. Still, it is important to remember

that even the most severe crisis, whether it be maturational or situational, can be a period of significant personality development for the
client.

Sometimes an individual or family will experience a stressful
situation that would put most other people into a state of crisis.
Yet for some reason, this particular individual or family is not thrown
into a crisis. Usually this occurs for one of two reasons. First,
the individual or family may not perceive the stressful event as a
life crisis. Instead, they may view the situation as a challenge and
go right on living determined to do even better. They may even accept
the crisis as an act of divine providence beyond their understanding
or control. Lindemann found this to be true of some families who had
lost a son or a daughter in the Coconut Grove Nightclub fire. On the
other hand, many people cope effectively as though it is not a crisis
because there are important life goals they still need to accomplish.
One of these life goals may be for a mother to set a strong example
for her four children despite her husband's death. Lindemann also
reported this situation in his study of bereavement. In addition,
Lindemann shows that people who resist crisis reactions because of
other impending demands usually experience delayed reactions weeks,
months, or even years after the loss of a spouse or a son or daughter.

In summary, whether or not a stressful event becomes a crisis
depends in large measure on how the individual or family perceives the
situation. If they do not see it as a hazard or a threat to important
life goals, they will usually not experience a crisis reaction. On
the other hand, if the stressful event is perceived as a crisis, they

will almost always suffer from a crisis reaction even though the crisis response may be delayed.

Treatment Conceptualization

Initial or Study Phase

In Paul's (1966a) article on "Crisis Intervention", he lists four tasks that the worker should complete during the initial stages of crisis treatment. Aguilera (1970b) also presents certain tasks for the crisis practitioner to accomplish. Accordingly, the writer believes that crisis workers should complete the six following tasks in the initial contact with the client:

1. Identify with the client the precipitating event.

2. Discuss how the client feels about the crisis.

3. Explore with the client how he has tried to cope with the crisis.

4. Assess whether or not the client can be helped on an outpatient basis.

5. Explain to the client why he is still in a state of crisis.

6. Begin discussing with the client tasks that he can accomplish in successfully resolving the crisis.

When the worker first meets with the client, it is imperative that he determine whether or not the client is in a state of crisis. Obviously, the presence of certain presenting symptoms would indicate that a crisis, in fact, exists. For example, Lindemann (1944, p. 10) found that clients experiencing the crisis of bereavement might be displaying one or more of the following symptoms: (1) somatic distress, (2) preoccupation with the image of the deceased, (3) guilt, (4) hostile reactions, and (5) loss of patterns of conduct. These symptoms are regarded as fairly characteristic of most crisis reactions, although depression and a sense of hopelessness are more common. However, these types of symptoms do not always indicate that the client is in a state of crisis. Bloom (1963), for instance, shows convincingly that even experts cannot always agree when a client is in crisis. In fact, Bloom reports that leading crisis experts could only agree a client was in a crisis if a precipitating stress or event could be clearly identified. This was even the case when other crisis symptoms such as depression were identified in the absence of a precipitating stress or event.

Consequently, it is recommended that the first task of the worker should be identifying with the client the precipitating stress that has led to the crisis. If the precipitating event can be clearly identified and the client is displaying symptoms characteristic of a crisis reaction, the worker can usually proceed on the assumption that the client is in a state of crisis. This initial crisis assessment is especially important because if the client is not in a crisis a more appropriate treatment plan, such as task-centered casework, should be considered.

After the precipitating stress has been identified, the worker needs to encourage the client to express his feelings about the crisis. This is important because the client often harbors intense feelings of guilt and hostility as well as remorse that need to be ventilated. In fact, unless this emotional catharsis takes place the client may not be able to sustain any movement. Rusk (1971, p. 255) believes this emotional release is essential for two reasons. First, it provides the worker with an appropriate opportunity to empathize with the client in his despair. Second, this emotional release induces appreciation in the client and marks the beginning of a therapeutic client-worker relationship. By encouraging the client to share his despair and frustration, the worker is showing that he cares about the client.

When the client has expressed how he feels about the crisis, the worker then begins exploring how the client has tried to deal with the problem. In particular, the worker needs information about what problem-solving activities and coping skills he has used and why they are failing. This task is important to accomplish if the worker hopes to gain a better understanding of the crisis. During this exploration, the worker needs to find out who besides the client is involved in the crisis and what role they are playing. This information will be extremely helpful in designing an effective treatment plan where all available resources are being used.

During this exploration, the worker also needs to determine whether or not the client can be helped on an outpatient basis. This assessment needs to be done quickly because crisis reactions can pose serious suicidal and homicidal risks. For example, some clients are so depressed that life does not seem worth living. In fact, as the worker explores how the client has tried to deal with the crisis, the client may imply or even say that he is tired of trying. Such clients may present serious suicidal risks and emergency hospitalization along with crisis care may be the treatment of choice. If for any reason the worker feels a suicidal or homicidal risk may exist, he should consider carefully the advisability of outpatient care. In situations such as these, the worker often consults with other staff members before a final decision is made.

When this initial exploration is completed, the worker helps the client understand why he is in a state of crisis. In particular, the worker guides him in not only identifying what precipitated the crisis but also in understanding why he has not yet been able to resolve the problem. Consider, for example, a husband who has lost his wife in an automobile accident. Because of this deep personal loss, the husband may experience an immediate crisis reaction. Yet the severity of his crisis reaction may be compounded by the stark realization that he also has four motherless children to care for. Many husbands who find themselves in similar crisis situations just do not know where to begin. Not only must they cope with the loss of their mates, they must also begin to meet the maternal needs of their children. It is no wonder they usually feel depressed and hopelessly lost. The worker needs to acknowledge this sense of loss and frustration with the client. In fact, the worker needs to let the client know that most people faced with similar problems would be reacting in the same way. As the client begins to understand why he is experiencing a crisis reaction, he usually does not feel as confused or as out of control. In addition, he continues to see the worker as a helpful person who has guided him in gaining a better understanding of what is happening to him.

At this stage in the initial contact, the worker lets the client know that his crisis can be successfully resolved. Many times the worker can begin instilling this sense of hope by referring to other

clients who have resolved similar crises. This can be especially
helpful to the client because it gives him an actual example of what
can be done. Still, the most effective message of help is a firm
pledge by the worker that he will help the client resolve his crisis.
Normally, most crisis reactions are resolved for better or for worse
in six to eight weeks. However, this does not mean that this six to
eight week period should be the basis of treatment although crisis
intervention is a time-limited intervention plan. Instead, the worker's
contract with the client should be based on the resolution of his crisis
whether or not it takes six to eight weeks. It is hoped, of course,
that the client's crisis will be resolved much sooner.

Once this contract has been forged, it is imperative that the
worker begin exploring with the client what can now be done to resolve
the crisis. Many times the best place to start is where the client
seems to be struggling the most. For example, a husband who has just
lost his wife now has to provide care for four small children. Although
his wife's death is a deep personal loss, he is faced with the immediate
task of meeting the needs of his children. This can be particularly
difficult if he does not have any close relatives in town who could
help him with the children. Consequently, the worker may begin exploring
with the client what alternatives are open to him. If the client cannot
call upon relatives or close friends for support, the worker may suggest
a temporary home-making service for the children until a more permanent
solution can be found. Whatever is done, it is important that the worker
show the client that help is on its way. After the initial contact is
completed, subsequent meetings with the client will focus on additional

tasks and problem-solving activities that will be helpful in resolving
the crisis.

In summary, the initial contact with the client is probably the
most crucial part of crisis intervention. During this initial meeting,
the worker must show through his words and actions that help is forthcoming and the crisis can be successfully resolved. This can best be
done by encouraging all crisis practitioners to complete six treatment
tasks during the initial interview. Since these six tasks are rather
inclusive, it is doubtful that the worker can complete them in the
traditional 50-minute hour. In fact, the writer believes the 50-minute
hour has no place in crisis treatment. Many times the worker may need
two or three hours to accomplish these six tasks. Such time is well
spent if the client emerges feeling that his crisis can be successfully
resolved.

Assessment or Diagnosis Phase

There is no designated assessment or diagnostic phase in crisis
intervention. Instead, assessment and diagnosis are ongoing parts of
crisis practice that permeate all stages of treatment. Consequently,
most crisis practitioners do not develop comprehensive diagnostic
assessments of the client. This is based on two reasons. First, crisis
theory is based on the assumption that before the crisis occurred the
client was functioning normally. In other words, crisis intervention
is not a treatment plan for chronic pathological problems such as long-
term alcoholism or schizophrenia. Instead, crisis practice is designed
to help normal functioning people who find themselves in crisis situa-

tions. Second, there is no time for a detailed or lengthy diagnostic study in crisis practice because the client needs help now. If the worker spends too much time worrying about diagnostic labels and personality functioning, he may be too late in giving the client the appropriate help when he needs it.

However, this does not mean that assessment or diagnosis is not used in crisis practice. Earlier the writer listed six tasks that the worker needs to accomplish in the initial interview. Each of these tasks requires the worker to make an assessment of what is happening to the client. For example, the first task was identifying with the client the precipitating stress that led to the crisis. Many times the client will be so depressed and despondent that it is difficult to locate a precipitating stress. On the other hand, the client may have experienced so many crisis provoking incidents that it is hard for the worker to identify which one is most important. Whatever the situation may be, the worker must assess and diagnose what is causing the crisis reaction.

During the accomplishment of the next two crisis tasks, the worker discusses with the client how he feels about his problem and what he has tried to do about it. Here assessment becomes most important since this exploration will reveal important information about the client's ego functioning and problem-solving skills. In fact, this information about the client's social functioning will give the worker an idea of what the client can and cannot do for himself in resolving his crisis. Obviously, this information will be vital in designing treatment strategies for the client. As the worker completes

the other tasks of the initial interview, he will continually make
assessments of what is happening to the client and how he can best
help.

Even so, one assessment must be made by all crisis practitioners
during this first meeting. Without exception, all crisis workers must
decide whether or not the client can be helped on an outpatient basis.
If they do not, they run the risk of further jeopardizing the welfare
of the client since crisis reactions can lead to suicidal and homicidal
risks. But in making this assessment, what diagnostic tool should the
worker use? In reviewing numerous crisis theorists, there are almost
as many diagnostic tools as authors. One author may use a psychoanalytic scheme while other practitioners feel Erikson's theory of developmental psychology is better. In the writer's judgment, any reasonably
developed theory of human behavior can be used by the worker as an
ongoing assessment tool. The writer prefers to use Erikson's theory
of developmental psychology because it shows how adaptive or maladaptive
ego mechanisms can either enhance or detract from personality development.
Other theories of human behavior can also be used as an assessment tool.
In using these theories of human behavior, however, it is important that
the crisis practitioner have a working knowledge of the theory as a
diagnostic tool.

In the psychoanalytic model, the therapist's diagnosis usually
leads to a detailed treatment plan that is designed to alleviate the
underlying personality disorders that are supposedly causing the
symptoms. Consequently, the therapist may spend months working with
the patient. In crisis intervention, the worker's primary concern is

helping the client resolve his crisis. Accordingly, when the client's crisis symptoms have disappeared treatment is generally terminated. If during the course of treatment the worker suspects underlying pathological malfunctioning, he normally refers the client for further counseling but only after the crisis reaction has reached some equilibrium. In other words, crisis practice is a time-limited treatment plan designed to restore the client to at least his pre-crisis level of functioning. But how does the worker do this? What treatment strategies can he use?

Most crisis theorists present one of two different treatment strategies. Jacobsen (1968) refers to them as the generic and individual approaches to crisis intervention. The central thesis of the generic approach is that for each different crisis reaction there are certain psychological tasks and problem-solving activities that every person must complete if he is to resolve successfully the crisis. In other words, in the generic approach there is no attempt to assess the individual needs of the client. Rather, the treatment focuses on the course a particular type of crisis characteristically follows with all clients. Consequently, generic crisis intervention offers a treatment plan designed for all clients experiencing the same crisis regardless of their individual differences. The individual approach, in comparison, focuses on the specific psychological tasks and problem-solving activities that each client must accomplish in resolving his crisis. Therefore, there are no predetermined tasks that every client must accomplish. Instead, the worker's treatment plan concentrates on each client's separate needs.

In formulating guidelines for crisis treatment plans, the writer has used the best of both the generic and individual approaches. To begin with, the writer feels any crisis treatment plan must meet the individual needs of the client. Consequently, the worker must be able to assess the needs of the client and design an appropriate treatment strategy. However, there are so many different types of crises that the worker needs some guidelines to follow in treatment. Therefore, it is proposed that when a generic approach exists for a specific crisis, the worker follow that pre-determined treatment plan adjusting it to the individual needs of the client. In other words, if the worker is helping a client suffering from the crisis of bereavement, he should follow a proven treatment plan such as the one proposed by Lindemann (1944). Yet in following a pre-determined treatment plan, the worker should make whatever adjustments are necessary to meet the individual needs of the client.

Crisis theorists have already devised treatment strategies for many specific crisis reactions. Therefore, it is imperative that crisis workers be familiar with the professional literature in crisis intervention. In fact, it is strongly recommended that the directors of all crisis intervention facilities should have a catalogued library of crisis literature. In addition, someone on the staff should be assigned the task of compiling a source book that outlines as many different crisis situations as possible and the corresponding psychological tasks and problems-solving activities suggested in resolving each crisis. This source book would be an invaluable guide in helping workers develop more effective treatment strategies.

Treatment Implementation

     Earlier, the writer described six tasks that the worker needs
to complete during the initial crisis interview. The last task focuses
on specific problem-solving activities that the client can begin
accomplishing in resolving the crisis. For example, Lindemann (1944,
p. 147) believes any client in the crisis of bereavement should complete
the following tasks or problem-solving activities:

    1. Accept the pain of bereavement.

    2. Review his relationship with the deceased and become
        acquainted with the alterations in his own modes of
        emotional release.

    3. Express sorrow and sense of loss.

    4. Find an acceptable formulation of his future relationships
        to the deceased.

    5. Verbalize his feelings of guilt and find persons around
        him whom he can use as "primers" for the acquisition of
        new patterns of conduct.

This list of psychological tasks is deemed appropriate for most clients
in the crisis of bereavement as long as the worker makes whatever
adjustments may be necessary in better meeting the individual needs of
each client. In other words, as crisis treatment continues the worker
needs to assess the appropriateness of each pre-determined task and the
client's ability to complete it.

     Where crisis theorists have not suggested specific psycholog-
ical tasks, the worker will have to construct his own based on the needs
of each client. However, there is a general treatment guideline the
worker can follow. Since many crisis reactions involve a significant
loss, the worker can often base his treatment plan on three general

tasks. First of all, the client needs to recognize the loss and express how he feels about it. Then he needs to explore with the worker how that loss can be compensated. Finally, the client needs to implement some activity that will compensate for the loss. This is exactly what Lindemann (1944) proposed in resolving the crisis of bereavement.

In implementing these psychological tasks and problem-solving activities, it is suggested that the worker use a systematic communication model such as the one presented by Reid and Epstein (1972, pp. 121-138) in their book Task-Centered Casework. In using this model, the worker focuses the client's communication on the psychological tasks he must complete in resolving the crisis. According to Reid and Epstein (1972, p. 23), these specific types of communication include:

1. Exploration of the client's problem, task possibilities, and task-related behavior.

2. Structuring the treatment relationship and communication within it.

3. Enhancing the client's awareness in ways to help him overcome obstacles to, or otherwise facilitate, task achievement.

4. Encouragement of task-directed behavior.

5. Suggesting means of task accomplishment.

Although this communication model is designed for task-centered casework, the writer believes it can also be used in crisis treatment to facilitate the completion of psychological tasks and the resolution of the crisis. In fact, most crisis practitioners likely already use these same communication skills in crisis intervention although no one has conceptualized a model as clearly as have Reid and Epstein.

Fox and Scherl (1972, pp. 37-42) demonstrate effectively the use of certain communication skills in helping 13 women resolve the crisis of rape. After a rape victim has been assaulted, her feelings usually include shock, disbelief, and dismay followed by anxiety and fear. Consequently, it is extremely important for her to talk about the assault. At this initial stage of crisis treatment, communication skills become extremely important. For example, if the rape victim is having a difficult time expressing how she feels about the assault, the worker can use active listening skills such as reflection to encourage her expression of feeling. As the victim begins expressing her sense of shock and disbelief, the worker can respond with empathy and warmth. This sincere expression of concern lets her know that someone cares. In addition, she begins seeing the worker as someone who understands and can help her in resolving the crisis. This, of course, is the beginning of a therapeutic client-worker relationship that hopefully extends through the entire treatment process.

After the client has expressed his feelings about the crisis, communication skills continue to be an important part of the treatment process. For instance, in the final stage of crisis treatment, the rape victim needs to express her feelings about herself and the assailant. During the earlier stages of treatment, most rape victims deny this need. However, a specific incident usually occurs late in treatment that uncovers this need. Often the victim is thrown into another crisis reaction when she learns she is pregnant or when she meets a man who resembles her assailant. It is at this time that the worker encourages her to speak of herself and the assailant. Many times the victim still

feels guilty or unclean but before the worker can reassure her she
must talk about these feelings. In addition, she may also be harboring
her anger toward the attacker. If she does not express these angry
feelings and examine there consequences, her future relationships with
other men may be seriously damaged. Consequently, the worker needs to
use exploration, support, encouragement, suggestion, and other communication skills in guiding the rape victim through these final crisis
resolving tasks.

To this point in the discussion, the theory of crisis intervention presented puts the worker in a directive role. This is probably
justified for two important reasons. First, crisis intervention is
a time-limited treatment with the central goal of helping the client
resolve his crisis successfully. In order to do this within a limited
time frame, the worker needs to guide the client. Second, crisis
practitioners have shown conclusively that if any crises are to be
resolved successfully, the client must complete certain psychological
tasks and problem-solving activities. In fact, the worker is profes-
sionally obligated to see that the client does complete these tasks.
Consequently, the worker uses a variety of communication skills along
with environmental supports to direct the client toward the completion
of these tasks.

Before discussing the final phase of crisis treatment, the writer
wants to make one point very clear. What the worker can do to help the
client resolve a crisis should not be restricted by any agency policy.
In fact, the worker should use whatever resources might be available
in the community to help the client. For example, if a father of

four is out of work and unable to meet his family's needs, the worker
needs to do more than just talk about the father's feelings. He needs
a free hand in searching out other community resources that can help
the father feed his family and eventually find a job. Consequently,
all crisis intervention agencies need to develop collateral contacts
with as many different community resources as possible. If they do
not, their crisis services will be severely limited.

The final stage of crisis treatment focuses on the termination
of client services. In the review of the crisis literature, it was
found that most authors tend to gloss over this final phase of treatment.
In fact, only a select few of the crisis theorists present any criteria
that helps the worker assess when termination is appropriate. In the
writer's judgment, crisis treatment should be terminated when the client
has successfully completed the psychological tasks associated with the
particular crisis. In addition, crisis services should be terminated
only when the client has also reached some state of equilibrium in his
social functioning. Although most clients will reach a more adequate
state of social functioning as they complete certain psychological
tasks, it is conceivable that a more appropriate level of behavior will
not result from the completion of these tasks. Fox and Scherl (1972)
found this to be true of most rape victims who were reluctant to
continue talking about the crisis once treatment began. Yet, this
temporary "flight into health" was suddenly stopped when the victim
found out she was pregnant or when she saw a man who resembled her
assailant. Consequently, it is imperative that the worker be alert to
this period of temporary adjustment since it usually leads to more

crucial treatment considerations.

    If the termination of crisis services focuses on the completion of certain tasks, the worker needs to prepare the client for the conclusion of treatment in advance. Usually this is best done in the initial contact when the worker explains that the client's crisis will be resolved by completing certain tasks and problem-solving activities. Then as the client continues to complete these tasks, the worker suggests to the client that in a few sessions he will have resolved his crisis. In other words, termination becomes an important part of crisis treatment that marks not only the completion of services but also the successful resolution of the client's crisis. When introduced in this manner, the client sees termination as the worker's signal that the client is ready to resume a normal life because the crisis is over.

    In the writer's opinion, one of the most crucial aspects of termination is what Aguilera (1970b, p. 17) refers to as anticipatory guidance. During this final phase of treatment, the worker reinforces those coping skills and problem-solving activities that the client has successfully used in resolving the crisis. This is important because it gives the client the opportunity to review what he has done in treatment. In addition, anticipatory guidance is important because it helps the client prepare for any future crises that he may encounter. In fact, through anticipatory guidance the client makes realistic plans for the future and anticipates how his newly acquired skills will enable him to function even better than before. Fox and Scherl (1972) present an interesting example of how anticipatory guidance can help rape victims separate their feelings toward the assailant from future relationships with other men.

During this phase of anticipatory guidance, the worker also assesses with the client the need for additional treatment after the crisis services are terminated. This need for additional treatment is usually not necessary unless the worker has identified chronic patterns of personality dysfunctioning that could prevent the client from achieving a more adequate level of social behavior. Collateral referrals can also be made if the worker believes the client still needs some support even though the crisis has been successfully resolved.

The final phase of termination deals with what Rapoport (1967, p. 40) identifies as the "open door" concept. At this time, the client is encouraged by the worker, and the agency he represents, to return for further help should the need arise. In other words, it is the worker's way of saying that the client's well-being is so important that the worker will be glad to assist him at any time. In addition, it conveys to the client that the relationship he has shared with the worker has not ended but it still available when needed. This is important since a therapeutic client-worker relationship is a meaningful experience for both parties.

Crisis Intervention Research

A Lack of Empirical Evidence

It has previously been shown that the research findings in crisis intervention are quite limited. This is probably the case for two important reasons. First, most crisis theorists have not developed models of crisis intervention that can be rigorously tested. Usually their models are too abbreviated to conceptualize clearly the distinguishing characteristics of crisis intervention as opposed to other treatment models. Consequently, it is most difficult for a practitioner to follow systematically such poorly conceptualized treatment plans. Accordingly, any outcome research by crisis theorists who have not conceptualized their crisis treatment plan is open to legitimate criticism.

Fortunately, a few crisis theorists have developed treatment plans that can be empirically tested. In fact, considerable outcome research has already been completed by Langsley (1968a, 1968b, 1969) and Kaplan (1968) in family crisis therapy at the Colorado Psychiatric Hospital. In their research, Langsley and Kaplan first present a detailed theory of treatment for families in crisis. Then they add documentation that this crisis intervention plan was used in helping families in crisis. Finally, they use expert clinicians not involved in their program to assess the treatment outcome of crisis practice. In so doing, Langsley and Kaplan present reliable research data that indicates crisis intervention is more successful with families in crisis than more traditional forms of treatment.

Still, the quality of most research in crisis intervention is poor. But what can be done to make it more effective? It is hoped this question will be answered in the following discussion.

Crisis Research Today

Most of the research done by crisis theorists focuses on the characteristics of the crisis reaction. In these research projects, the authors usually observe people in crisis and record their subsequent behavior. The classic example of this type of exploratory research is Lindemann's (1944) pioneering study on bereavement. From these exploratory research studies, theorists such as Caplan (1964, 1965) have constructed models in which they describe the nature of the crisis reaction. Other crisis theorists such as Bloom (1963), Parad (1960, 1962, 1968, 1971), and Rapoport (1962a, 1962b, 1967, 1970) have added to this understanding of the crisis reaction. Consequently, present theory includes a clear conceptualization of the crisis reaction along with its characteristic types and stages.

In comparison, most crisis theorists have been less thorough in conceptualizing crisis practice. In the writer's judgment, this is the area in which crisis theorists need to concentrate their efforts. Unfortunately, many crisis researchers do not see this same need because they continue to spend valuable research time and money duplicating earlier studies that describe the nature of the crisis reaction. A good example of this unnecessary duplication of earlier crisis research is La Sor (1970) and Strickler's article on "The Concept of Loss in Crisis Intervention". Although they try to present a new conceptualization of loss, their findings are basically the same as those Lindemann reported in 1944.

In the writer's judgment, crisis theorists need to sharpen their conceptualizations of crisis practice. Some crisis authors are already doing this. In fact, during the last five years most researchers have attempted to describe how crisis intervention is used in a variety of practice settings. In all but a few of these practice areas, the writer has found that most theorists present sketchy conceptualizations of crisis treatment that are difficult to follow let alone empirically test. As crisis theorists continue to clarify the essential features of practice, they will help practitioners by providing guidelines to treatment based on accepted principles of crisis intervention. When this point is reached, researchers will be better able to assess the effectiveness of crisis practice.

Research Needs for Tomorrow

Social work and all other helping professions are facing an evaluation crisis. In one instance, this crisis has arisen because of our inability or unwillingness to assess the effectiveness of our treatment program. On the other hand, part of the problem persists because evaluations have raised doubts as to the efficacy of any intervention programs. In the writer's opinion, crisis theorists are caught in this same dilemma because most of them have not shown through sound empirical research that crisis intervention is successful. However, before evaluation research can be conducted, crisis theorists need to specify further the nature of practice and then train practitioners who can effectively apply the treatment strategies. Once they have completed these two steps, they will be in a better position to assess the effectiveness of crisis practice.

Langsley (1968a, 1968b, 1969) and Kaplan (1968) have already completed these two steps as shown by their research in family crisis treatment. In fact, the writer feels their evaluative research model can serve as a guide for other crisis theorists who are interested in assessing treatment outcome. For instance, both authors begin by presenting clear conceptualizations of family crisis treatment that are already being used by experienced practitioners. Only then do they attempt to assess the effectiveness of crisis treatment.

At this point in their research, they discuss how the random assignment of families to different treatment programs helps to ensure accurate research results. Consequently, they randomly assign 75 families to their crisis treatment program and 75 to the more tradition-al hospital psychiatric services. This random selection is important because it increases the chances that both treatment programs will have a similar sampling of clients, thereby reducing the possibilities of client bias. In fact, most crisis theorists continue to use random sampling in strengthening their research designs. This is a sound approach since research authorities such as Campbell and Stanley (1972) state that this is the most effective way to control for client bias.

After the families had been randomly assigned to different treatment groups, Langsley and Kaplan had to be sure that the data they collected from these two groups were accurate. In particular, they were interested in verifying that the practitioners in each of these treatment groups were following their respective treatment models. Consequently, they recorded on tape the treatment sessions and asked all the practitioners to keep detailed records of what they were doing with their clients. In this way, they could periodically determine whether or not the crisis practitioners were following accepted princi-ples of crisis treatment. Satisfied that the workers were following accepted principles of crisis treatment, Langsley and Kaplan were now in a position to assess treatment outcome.

In assessing treatment outcome, the authors used certain accepted psychological tests along with the expert opinions of experienced clinicians who were not members of either treatment group. In so doing, they were able to show conclusively that crisis treatment was more successful and more durable than traditional psychiatric services in helping families in crisis. By using the expert opinions of experienced clinicians who did not know which families received crisis service, Langsley and Kaplan avoided one of the most common pitfalls of evaluative research — assessing the treatment outcome of your own clients. Even some of the leading crisis theorists (Caplan, 1960, 1965; Parad, 1960, 1968; Rapoport, 1962b) continue to make this same mistake, thereby casting doubt on the validity of their research findings because of possible worker bias. The chances of worker bias can be reduced by engaging other expert clinicians not associated with the research project in assessing treatment outcome.

In the preceding brief discussion of crisis research, an effort has been made to present some of the more crucial methodological considerations involved in conducting sound evaluative research. By following these suggestions, the researcher can better assess the effectiveness of crisis treatment. For those interested in a more complete discussion of evaluative research, the reader is referred to Campbell and Stanley (1972) and Selltiz (1959), who discuss in-depth some of the more important methodological problems.

Current Issues and Problems

More Than an Assessment Tool

Crisis intervention is both an assessment and treatment tool designed to help individuals and families in crisis. However, crisis intervention is not the treatment of choice for most problems of living where the client has been in conflict for some extended period of time. In these situations, a more inclusive treatment plan such as task-centered casework is more appropriate. However, when the client is struggling with a crisis reaction that has been precipitated by a hazardous event or a significant loss, crisis intervention remains the treatment of choice.

Today, crisis theorists have adapted their treatment plans to many different practice settings that serve children and adolescents, families, hospitals, etc. In addition, some authors, including Atkinson (1971) and Lundberg (1970), have used crisis concepts in helping military and governmental administrators deal more effectively with personnel conflicts. Accordingly, crisis intervention is no longer viewed as a "second-best" approach. Instead, theorists have developed treatment models that are beginning to demonstrate the effectiveness of crisis intervention.

Unresolved Issues and Problems

Despite these contributions, crisis theorists and practitioners are still struggling with some difficult problems. According to Rapoport (1970), the "most glaring problem is that there is little systematic practice that consciously uses the crisis model [p. 307]".

In other words, most crisis practitioners are not using accepted principles of crisis intervention in treatment. Unfortunately, the writer has also found this to be true after completing an extensive review of the crisis literature. In fact, most crisis theorists present sketchy conceptualizations of practice that even the most skilled clinician would have difficulty in following. The writer has attempted to solve this problem by presenting an extensive conceptualization of crisis treatment. As other authors continue to refine crisis treatment, it will be much easier to follow a systematic body of crisis practice based on accepted principles of crisis intervention.

Parad (1971, pp. 201-202) believes the problem is much broader than simply specifying crisis treatment and lists the following knowledge areas where exploratory research is desperately needed:

1. Criteria for intervention.

2. The client's perception of the precipitating stressful event.

3. Whether and why the worker and client think there is a crisis and how serious it is.

4. The goals of treatment in specific rather than global terms.

5. The client's and the worker's perceptions of the time dimension.

6. Types of treatment techniques used.

7. How the worker and the client perceive outcome both at the time of termination and at prearranged time intervals following intervention.

In examining this list, it is apparent that most of Parad's research suggestions are an attempt to clarify what characterizes crisis treatment. In fact, there seems to be no real difference between Rapoport's research suggestions and those of Parad other than the fact Parad attempts to identify specific treatment areas that remain unclear. Consequently, both theorists are saying that crisis treatment is still conceptually unclear and will probably remain so until more research is conducted.

The writer agrees with both authors. Yet before crisis treatment can be explored, theorists and practitioners must first take the time to conceptualize what constitutes crisis practice. In order to do this, they will need to identify and describe systematically the various aspects and stages of crisis treatment.

Conclusion

In this chapter, a general theory of crisis intervention that can hopefully be used across a variety of practice settings has been presented. At the present stage of development, the model is far from a complete conceptualization of crisis theory and practice. However, it does offer the practitioner a systematic and descriptive conceptualization of crisis intervention. In addition, the model helps the practitioner follow the process of crisis treatment from the initial contact through the termination of services. The real value of this general theory of crisis intervention will not be known until skilled practitioners use it in their crisis practice. At that time, certain gaps may well be located in the model. Still, these gaps will provide the writer and other crisis theorists with the opportunity of further clarifying the nature of crisis intervention. As this refinement continues, crisis intervention will more readily be acknowledged as the treatment of choice for individuals and families in crisis.

CHAPTER XVII

SUMMARY, CONCLUSIONS, AND RECOMMENDATIONS

Purpose

The purposes of this study were: (1) To review and compare the
various conceptual frameworks that have been used to describe crisis
intervention; (2) To examine and describe how these various conceptual
frameworks of crisis intervention have been operationalized into practice
and used with such selected problems of living as marital and family
conflicts, emergency hospitalization, suicide, etc.; (3) To analyze
the similarities and differences between these various conceptual
frameworks and practices of crisis intervention and planned short-term
treatment; (4) To develop a general conceptual framework for crisis
intervention that can be operationalized into practice across a variety
of problem areas.

Methodology

In completing these four research objectives, the study was
limited to an exhaustive research and review of the literature on
crisis intervention. Two major computer search programs offered
through the University of Utah library system were used in identifying
and retrieving the crisis literature that pertained to the stated
purposes of the study. Also employed was a library hand search of

various publications and articles dealing with crisis intervention up to and including December of 1972. This library hand search was completed by utilizing a number of different general reference indexes such as Psychological Abstracts. After the literature search was completed, 273 crisis articles and publications were located. In analyzing these 273 articles and publications, the study focused on an extensive assessment framework designed to yield data for each of the four objectives of the study. This same assessment framework was used in systematically reporting the findings of the study.

Findings

The study revealed that the most notable contributions to the theory and development of crisis intervention were made by the following authors: Erich Lindemann and Gerald Caplan, Lydia Rapoport, Howard J. Parad, Gerald F. Jacobsen, and Donna C. Aguilera. Of these six authors, the earlier contributions of Lindemann and Caplan remain the foundation of present-day crisis theory and practice.

A review of the contributions of these and other crisis theorists indicated that most crisis authors have conceptualized clearly the essential features of the crisis reaction. In fact, most theorists are still using Caplan's earlier definition of a crisis along with his characteristic stages of development. Unfortunately, most crisis theorists were less clear in their conceptualizations of crisis practice with the notable exceptions of Aguilera and Rapoport. Consequently, it was often difficult to see how crisis theory was operationalized into practice because the treatment models were so vague. Even today, most crisis theorists have not clearly operationalized crisis treatment.

The review of the crisis literature also indicated that crisis
practice focuses primarily on the five following areas: (1) childhood and
adolescent crises, (2) mental health problems, (3) marital and family
conflicts, (4) emergency hospitalization, and (5) suicide prevention.
Of these five practice areas, the model of Langsley and Kaplan for
families in crisis is probably the clearest conceptualization of crisis
treatment. In addition, these two authors have presented sound empirical
evidence to support their treatment claims. In comparison, most crisis
practitioners are still unclear in their conceptualizations of treatment
models. Consequently, any outcome research conducted by most crisis
practitioners is subject to criticism because of the sketchiness of the
treatment models being tested.

A comparison of crisis intervention with Reid and Epstein's
model of planned short-term treatment (task-centered casework), revealed
some important differences. To begin with, planned short-term treatment
can be adapted to more problems of living than crisis intervention.
In addition, planned short-term treatment is a much clearer model of
practice than crisis intervention. However, when the individual or
family is experiencing a crisis reaction that has been precipitated by
a hazardous event or a significant loss, crisis intervention remains
the accepted treatment of choice.

In conclusion, the study has also presented a general theory
of crisis intervention that can be adapted to most practice settings.
This crisis model presents the practitioner with a systematic and
descriptive conceptualization of crisis intervention. In addition, the

model is designed to help all crisis students to follow the stages of crisis practice from the initial contact through termination. This is important because most crisis treatment plans are limited to specific crisis reactions and are not intended to cover other crisis conflicts.

Conclusions

Based on the findings of this study, it seems reasonable to conclude that crisis intervention is not yet a conceptually clear model of social intervention. In fact, crisis theory and practice have not changed appreciably from the pioneering contributions of Lindemann and Caplan in the late 1940's and early 1950's. This seems to have occurred because most crisis authors have not operationalized crisis theory into clear conceptual treatment plans. Instead, their efforts have duplicated earlier research studies, especially around the characteristic stages of the crisis reaction. This research has been helpful in further clarifying what happens to an individual or a family in crisis. Yet these research studies have continued to focus only on this aspect of crisis intervention. Consequently, much of the current research and investigation in crisis intervention has become counter-productive because it has not added new knowledge to the field, particularly around crisis treatment. This is why Parad (1971, p. 201) has said that the crucial developmental task facing crisis theorists is to build up a cumulative body of knowledge rather than to settle for the largely repetitive one they now have.

One of the best ways of building up a cumulative body of crisis

knowledge is for theorists and practitioners to focus their efforts
on conceptualizing crisis treatment. In particular, they need to
describe the process of crisis treatment from the initial contact
through termination. Some crisis theorists have already done this.
In fact, the family crisis treatment model of Langsley and Kaplan is
probably the best conceptualization of crisis treatment available today.
As other theorists and practitioners take the time to conceptualize
their treatment models, researchers will be able to conduct better
studies on crisis practice. Consequently, crisis knowledge should
increase dramatically.

There are other areas besides crisis treatment in which new
knowledge is needed. For example, most crisis theorists feel that
much more research needs to be done on why clients perceive stressful
events as crises. Others feel that a person's socio-economic status
may influence how well he responds to crisis treatment. These and
other areas of research are needed. Yet if theorists and practitioners
try to answer these questions without first conceptualizing the nature
of crisis treatment, their effort will be less than productive because
they are, so to speak, "putting the cart before the horse". Unless
they first conceptualize crisis treatment and train skilled practitioners
in using this intervention, they will not be able to assess accurately
how a person's socio-economic status affects treatment or how countless
other client variables influence the effectiveness of crisis practice.

Recommendations

If the knowledge base and effectiveness of crisis intervention

are to be enhanced, crisis theorists and practitioners, along with the
agencies they represent, should seriously consider the following
recommendations:

1. It is recommended that crisis theorists and practitioners
develop models of crisis intervention that focus on the process of
treatment from the initial contact with the client or family through
termination of services.

2. It is recommended that in developing these treatment models
crisis theorists and practitioners use a conceptual framework such as
the ones developed by Briar and Miller (1971), Roberts and Nee (1972),
Vincent (1972), and the writer.

3. It is recommended that instead of developing treatment
models for specific crisis situations, theorists and practitioners
focus their efforts on a more general model of crisis intervention
that can be applied to most practice settings.

4. It is recommended that crisis theorists and practitioners
assess in various practice settings the usefulness of the writer's
general theory of crisis intervention.

5. It is recommended that any agency offering crisis intervention
services seriously consider implementing the following list of administrative policies suggested earlier by Parad (1971, p. 201):

    a. The elimination of waiting lists.

    b. The avoidance of complex intake screening so treatment
       will be simultaneous with diagnosis.

    c. The development of an open door policy for those who
       may require further services when faced with new crisis.

d. The use of a built-in policy of preplanned follow-up interviews to provide feedback about the effectiveness of services.

6. It is recommended that crisis intervention agencies maintain up-to-date library facilities that contain research, reviews, and pertinent articles and publications on crisis theory and practice.

7. It is recommended that these same agencies provide practitioners with treatment source books that discuss as many different crisis reactions as possible and the psychological tasks and problem-solving activities that are suggested in helping individuals and families successfully resolve these crises.

8. It is recommended that in-service training programs consider crisis intervention as a valuable treatment model in enhancing the clinical skills of staff members.

9. It is recommended that national, state, and local mental health programs and facilities consider adopting more extensive crisis intervention programs that can markedly increase services while reducing the cost and duration of treatment.

10. It is recommended that educational institutions engaged in the training of professional clinicians acknowledge crisis intervention as a recognized model of social intervention and implement specific courses to teach the crisis model.

11. It is recommended that in enriching the social work education curriculum crisis intervention content be included in relevant human behavior and social environment sequence courses for the benefit of all social work students.

12. It is recommended that students specializing in clinical practice complete the crisis intervention course.

13. It is recommended that all public and private treatment programs and facilities consider crisis intervention the treatment of choice for individuals and families in crisis.

14. It is recommended that crisis theorists and practitioners investigate how crisis intervention theory might be applied to larger systems such as groups, neighborhoods, communities, and even nations.

Bibliography

Ackerman, N. W. (Ed.) Family therapy in transition. Boston: Little,
Brown, & Company, 1970.

Aguilera, D. C. Crisis: Moment of truth, Journal of Psychiatric
Nursing and Mental Health Services, 1971, 9(3), 23-25.

Aguilera, D. C. Sociocultural factors: Barriers to therapeutic
intervention, Journal of Psychiatric Nursing and Mental Health
Services, 1970, 8(5), 14-18. (a)

Aguilera, D. C., Messick, J. M., and Farrell, M. S. Crisis intervention: Theory and methodology. St. Louis: The C. V. Mosby
Company, 1970. (b)

Aguilera, D. C., Messick, J. M., and Morley, W. E. Crisis intervention:
Paradigms of intervention, Journal of Psychiatric Nursing and
Mental Health Services, 1967, 5(6), 531-544.

Allgeyer, J. M. The crisis group — Its unique usefulness to the
disadvantaged, International Journal of Group Psychotherapy,
1970, 20(2), 235-240.

Appley, M. H., and Trumbull, R. Psychological stress. New York:
Appleton-Century-Crofts, 1967.

Argles, P., and Mackenzie, M. Crisis intervention with a multi-problem
family: A case study, Journal of Child Psychology and Psychiatry
and Allied Disciplines, 1970, 11(3), 187-195.

Armsby, R. E. The adolescent crisis team: An experiment in community
crisis intervention, Proceedings of the Convention of the
American Psychological Association, 1971, 6(2), 735-736.

Atherton, C. R., Mitchell, S. T., and Scheim, E. B. Locating points
for intervention, Social Casework, 1971, 52(3), 131-141.

Atkinson, R. M. Ineffective personnel in military service: A critique
of concepts and rehabilitation practices from a psychiatric
viewpoint, American Journal of Psychiatry, 1971, 127(12), 1612-
1618.

Bailey, D. Occupational therapy in a crisis intervention unit of a
large general hospital, Australian Occupational Therapy Journal,
1971, 18(4), 13-17.

Baldwin, K. A. Crisis-focused casework in a child guidance clinic,
Social Casework, 1968, 49(1), 28-34.

Balson, P. M. The use of behavior therapy techniques in crisis-intervention: A case report, Journal of Behavior Therapy and Experimental Psychiatry, 1971, 2(4), 297-300.

Barten, H. H. (Ed.) Brief therapies. New York: Behavioral Publications, Inc., 1971.

Beahan, L. T. Emergency mental health services in a general hospital, Hospital and Community Psychiatry, 1970, 21(3), 81-84.

Bellak, L., and Small, L. Emergency psychotherapy and brief psychotherapy. New York: Grune & Stratton, 1965.

Bennett, G. F. Pastoral care in psychiatric crisis, Pastoral Psychology, 1970, 21(205), 35-40.

Berlin, I. N. Crisis intervention and short-term therapy: An approach in a child-psychiatric clinic, Journal of the American Academy of Child Psychiatry, 1970, 9(4), 595-606.

Berliner, B. S. Nursing a patient in crisis, American Journal of Nursing, 1970, 70(10), 2154-2157.

Berstein, R. Are we still stereotyping the unmarried mother. In H. J. Parad (Ed.) Crisis intervention: Selected readings. New York: Family Service Association of America, 1965, Pp. 100-110.

Birley, J. L., and Brown, G. W. Crises and life changes preceding the onset or relapse of acute schizophrenia: Clinical aspects, British Journal of Psychiatry, 1970, 116, 327-333.

Black, K. M. Teaching family process and intervention, Nursing Outlook, 1970, 18(6), 54-58.

Blaufarb, H., and Levine, J. Crisis intervention in an earthquake, Social Work, 1972, 17(4), 16-19.

Block, H. S. Brief sleep treatment with chlorpromazine, Comprehensive Psychiatry, 1970, 11(4), 346-355.

Bloom, B. C. Definitional aspects of the crisis concept, Journal of Consulting Psychology, 1963, 27(6), 498-502.

Bonier, R. J., and Koplovsky, A. Borderline adolescent in crisis intervention, Proceedings of the Convention of the American Psychological Association, 1971, 6(1), 437-438.

Bonstedt, T. Crisis intervention or early access brief therapy? Diseases of the Nervous System, 1970, 31(11), 783-787.

Brandon, S. Crisis theory and possibilities of therapeutic intervention, British Journal of Psychiatry, 1970, 117(541), 627-633.

Briar, S., and Miller, H. Problems and issues in social casework. New York: Columbia University Press, 1971.

Brockopp, G. W. Crisis theory and suicide prevention, Crisis Intervention, 1970, 2(2, Suppl.), 38-41. (a)

Brockopp, G. W. A note on the telephone handling of the obscene caller, Crisis Intervention, 1970, 2(4), 96-98. (b)

Brockopp, G. W. The telephone call: Conversation or therapy, Crisis Intervention, 1970, 2(3), 73-75. (c)

Brockopp, G. W., and Yasser, A. Training the volunteer telephone therapist, Crisis Intervention, 1970, 2(3) 65-72. (d)

Brown, F. G. The zone concept in psychiatric care, American Journal of Nursing, 1969, 69(9), 1923-1926.

Brown, G. W., and Birley, J. L. T. Crises and life changes and the onset of schizophrenia, Journal of Health and Social Behavior, 1968, 9(3), 203-214.

Brown, H. F., Burditt, V. B., and Liddell, C. W. The crisis of relocation. In H. J. Parad (Ed.) Crisis intervention: Selected readings. New York: Family Service Association of America, 1965, Pp. 248-260.

Brown, T. E. Career counseling as a form of pastoral care, Pastoral Psychology, 1971, 22(212) 15-20.

Brown, V. B. Drug people: Schizoid personalities in search of a treatment, Psychotherapy, 1971, 8(3), 213-215.

Bryt, A. Emergency psychotherapeutic assistance, American Journal of Orthopsychiatry, 1962, 32(1), 399-403.

Burnside, I. M. Crisis intervention with geriatric hospitalized patients, Journal of Psychiatric Nursing and Mental Health Services, 1970, 8(2), 17-20.

Cain, A. C., and Fast, I. Children's disturbed reactions to parent suicide, American Journal of Orthopsychiatry, 1966, 36(5), 873-880.

Campbell, D. T., and Stanley, J. C. Experimental and quasi-experimental designs for research. Chicago: Rand McNally & Company, 1972.

Cannon, W. B. The wisdom of the body. New York: W. W. Norton & Company, 1967.

Caplan, G. Patterns of parental response to the crisis of premature birth: A preliminary approach to modifying the mental-health outcome, Psychiatry, 1960, 23(4), 365-374.

Caplan, G. Principles of preventive psychiatry. New York: Basic Books, Inc., 1964.

Caplan, G., Mason, E., and Kaplan, D. Four studies of crisis in parents of prematures, Community Mental Health Journal, 1965, 1(2), 149-161.

Carpenter, W. T., Tamarkin, N. R., and Raskin, D. E. Emergency psychiatric treatment during a mass rally: The march on washington, American Journal of Psychiatry, 1971, 127(10), 1327-1332.

Casse, R. M. Use of a "freak out" control center, Journal of College Student Personnel, 1970, 11(6), 403-408.

Cath, S. H. Some dynamics of the middle and later years. In H. J. Parad (Ed.) Crisis intervention: Selected readings. New York: Family Service Association of America, 1965, Pp. 174-192.

Cattell, J. P. Psychiatric emergencies in general practice: Reassessment, New York State Journal of Medicine, 1970, 70(17), 2219-2223.

Char, W. F., and McDermott, J. F., Jr. Abortions and acute identity crisis in nurses, American Journal of Psychiatry, 1972, 128(8), 952-957.

Chaskel, R. Assertive casework in a short-term situation. In H. J. Parad (Ed.) Crisis intervention: Selected readings. New York: Family Service Association of America, 1965, Pp. 237-247.

Clark, E. Round-the-clock emergency psychiatric services. Social work practice, 1963: Papers from the national conference on social welfare. New York: Columbia University Press, 1963, Pp. 44-57.

Clarke, J. An analysis of crisis management by mental welfare officers, British Journal of Social Work, 1971, 1(1), 27-37.

Cohen, R. E., and Schulberg, H. C. A review and preview of a training program in community mental health, Community Mental Health Journal, 1970, 6(5), 383-386.

Cohen, S. I., and Walder, L. O. An experimental analog derived from crisis theory, American Journal of Orthopsychiatry, 1971, 41(5) 822-829.

Coleman, M. D., and Zwerling, T. The psychiatric emergency clinic:
A flexible way of meeting community mental health needs,
American Journal of Psychiatry, 1959, 115(11), 980-984.

Confer, C. E. Operation crisis, Lutheran Social Welfare Quarterly,
1968, 8(1), 5-16.

Cowen, L. Anxiety, self-concept, and the semantic differential,
Journal of Psychology, 1972, 80(1), 65-68.

Crary, W. G. Goals and techniques of transitory group therapy,
Hospital and Community Psychiatry, 1968, 19(12), 389-391.

Crary, W. G., and Johnson, C. W. Attitude therapy in a crisis-intervention program, Hospital and Community Psychiatry, 1970, 21(5),
165-168.

Cumming, J., and Cumming, E. Ego and milieu. New York: Atherton
Press, 1963.

Cyr, F. E., and Wattenberg, S. H. Social work in a preventive program
of maternal and child health. In H. J. Parad (Ed.) Crisis
intervention: Selected readings. New York: Family Service
Association of America, 1965, Pp. 88-99.

DaCell, L. A. International hotline survery: A preliminary report,
Proceedings of the Convention of the American Psychological
Association, 1972, 7(Pt. 2), 807-808.

Darbonne, A. Crisis: A review of theory, practice, and research,
International Journal of Psychiatry, 1968, 6(5), 371-377.

Darley, J. M., and Latane, B. When will people help in a crisis?
Psychology Today, 1968, 2(7), 54-57, 70-71.

Decker, J. B., and Stubblebine, J. M. Crisis intervention and prevention
of psychiatric disability: A follow-up study, American Journal
of Psychiatry, 1972, 129(6), 725-729.

Deeths, A. Psychodrama crisis intervention with delinquent male drug
users, Group Psychotherapy and Psychodrama, 1970, 23(1-2),
41-44.

Dension, J. M. An unusual social experiment to help youth in crisis,
Canadian Medical Association Journal, 1971, 104(1), 15-19.

De Young, C. D., et. al. The treatment of families in crisis. New
York: Grune and Stratton, 1968.

Dinoff, M., Finch, A. J., and Clements, C. B. Testing clinical judgment
during a crisis, Psychological Reports, 1970, 26(1), 181-182.

Duckworth, G. L. A project in crisis intervention, Social Casework, 1967, 48(4), 227-231.

Dyer, E. D. Parenthood as crises: A re-study, Marriage and Family Living, 1963, 25(2), 196-201.

Ehrlich, P. R., and Ehrlich, A. H. Population, resources, environment: Issues in human ecology. San Francisco: W. H. Freeman, 1970.

Eisendrath, R. M. The role of grief and fear in the death of kidney transplant patients, American Journal of Psychiatry, 1969, 126 (3), 381-387.

Eisler, R. M., and Hersen, M. Behavioral techniques in family-oriented crisis intervention, Archives of General Psychiatry, 1973, 28(1), 111-116.

Epstein, L. Casework process in crisis abatement, Child Welfare, 1965, 44(10), 551-555, 562.

Erikson, E. H. Childhood and society. New York: W. W. Norton and Company, 1950.

Erikson, E. H. Growth and crisis of the healthy personality. In C. Kluckhohn and H. Murray (Eds.) Personality in nature, society, and culture. New York: Alfred Knopf, 1956, Pp. 185-225.

Errera, P., Wyshak, G., and Jarecki, H. Psychiatric care in a general hospital emergency room, Archives of General Psychiatry, 1963, 9, 105-112.

Farberow, N. L. Ten years of suicide prevention -- Past and future, Bulletin of Suicidology, 1970, 6(Spring), 6-11.

Farberow, N. L., and Shneidman, E. S. (Eds.) The cry for help. New York: McGraw-Hill, 1961.

Farnsworth, D. L., and Braceland, F. J. (Eds.) Psychiatry, the clergy and pastoral counseling: The st. john's story. Collegeville: St. John's University Press, 1969.

Ferguson, R. D. Consider crisis intervention. Unpublished working paper, University of Utah, June, 1973.

Fischer, J. Is casework effective? A review, Social Work, 1973, 18(1), 5-20.

Flint, A. A. Crisis in marriage — reification or reality? American Journal of Orthopsychiatry, 1968, 38(3), 560-564.

Flomenhaft, K., Kaplan, D. M., and Langsley, D. G. Avoiding psychiatric hospitalization, Social Work, 1969, 14(4), 38-45.

Florell, J. L. Crisis intervention in orthopedic surgery, Dissertation Abstracts International, 1971, 32(6-B), 3633.

Foreman, N. J., and Zerwekh, J. V. Drug crisis intervention, American Journal of Nursing, 1971, 71(9), 1736-1739.

Forer, B. The therapeutic value of crises, Psychological Reports, 1963, 13(1), 275-281.

Fox, S. S., and Scherl, D. J. Crisis intervention with victims of rape, Social Work, 1972, 17(1), 37-42.

Fredrick, C. J., and Resnick, H. L. Interventions with suicidal patients, Journal of Contemporary Psychotherapy, 1970, 2(2), 103-109.

Freeman, E. H., et. al. Assessing patient characteristics from psychotherapy interviews. In H. J. Parad (Ed.) Crisis intervention: Selected readings. New York: Family Service Association of America, 1965, Pp. 349-365.

Galdston, R., and Hughes, M. C. Pediatric hospitalization as crisis intervention, American Journal of Psychiatry, 1972, 129(6), 721-725.

Garrell, D. C. A hotline telephone service for young people in crisis, Children, 1969, 16(5), 177-180.

Gebbie, K. M. Treatment drop-outs and the role of the crisis therapist, Journal of Psychiatric Nursing and Mental Health Services, 1968, 6(6), 328-333.

Glasser, P. H., and Glasser, L. N. (Eds.) Families in crisis. New York: Harper and Row, 1970.

Glasser, W. Reality therapy. New York: Harper & Row, Publishers, 1965.

Golan, N. When is a client in crisis? Social Casework, 1969, 50(7), 389-394.

Gottschalk, L. A., et. al. Prediction and evaluation of outcome in an emergency brief psychotherapy clinic, Journal of Nervous and Mental Disease, 1967, 144(2), 77-96.

Greer, S., and Bagley, C. Effect of psychiatric intervention in attempted suicide: A controlled study, British Medical Journal, 1971, 1(5744), 310-312.

Grey, A. L., and Dermody, H. E. Reports of casework failure, Social Casework, 1972, 53(9), 534-543.

Hall, C. S., and Lindzey, G. Theories of personality. New York: John Wiley & Sons, Inc., 1970.

Halpern, H. A. Crisis: A definitional study, Dissertation Abstracts International, 1971, 32(2-B), 1212.

Harris, M. R., Kallis, B., and Freeman, E. Precipitating stress: An approach to brief therapy, American Journal of Psychotherapy, 1963, 17(3), 465-471.

Hart, T. F. The changing function of the london girls' remand home: Crisis -- Intervention and classification, International Journal of Offender Therapy, 1971, 15(1), 35-47.

Hartman, H. Ego psychology and the problem of adaptation. New York: International Universities Press, 1958.

Hecker, A. O., and Wright, E. R. Reassessing hospital treatment practices, Hospital and Community Psychiatry, 1968, 19(11), 362-363.

Heilig, S. M., and Klugman, D. J. The social worker in a suicide prevention center. In H. J. Parad (Ed.) Crisis intervention: Selected readings. New York: Family Service Association of America, 1965, Pp. 274-283.

Hiatt, C. C., and Spurlock, R. E. Geographical flight and its relation to crisis theory, American Journal of Orthopsychiatry, 1970, 40(1), 53-57.

Hill, R. Families under stress. New York: Harper & Brothers, Publishers, 1949.

Hill, R. Generic features of families under stress, Social Casework, 1958, 39(2-3), 139-149.

Hollis, F. Casework: A psychosocial therapy. New York: Random House, 1964.

Hurwitz, J. I., Kaplan, D. M., and Kaiser, E. Designing an instrument to assess parental coping mechanisms. In H. J. Parad (Ed.) Crisis intervention: Selected readings. New York: Family Service Association of America, 1965, Pp. 339-348.

Ichikawa, A. Observations of college students in acute distress. In H. J. Parad (Ed.) Crisis intervention: Selected readings. New York: Family Service Association of America, 1965, Pp. 167-173.

Irvine, E. E. Children at risk. In H. J. Parad (Ed.) Crisis intervention: Selected readings. New York: Family Service Association of America, 1965, Pp. 220-226.

Jacobsen, G. F. Crisis intervention from the viewpoint of the mental health professional, Pastoral Psychology, 1970, 21(203), 21-28.

Jacobsen, G. F. Crisis theory and treatment strategy: Some sociocultural and psychodynamic considerations, Journal of Nervous and Mental Disease, 1965, 141(2), 209-217. (a)

Jacobsen, G. F. Some psychoanalytic considerations regarding crisis therapy, Psychoanalytic Review, 1965, 141(2), 25-31. (b)

Jacobsen, G. F., Strickler, M., and Morley, W. Generic and individual approaches to crisis intervention, American Journal of Public Health, 1968, 58(1), 338-343.

Janis, I. L. Psychological stress. New York: John Wiley & Sons, Inc., 1958.

Johnson, D. W. Students against the school establishment: Crisis intervention in school conflicts and organizational change, Journal of School Psychology, 1971, 9(1), 84-92.

Juechter, J. K. Guidelines for suicide prevention in new york state colleges, Dissertation Abstracts International, 1971, 32(5-A), 2307.

Kaffman, M. Short-term family therapy. In H. J. Parad (Ed.) Crisis intervention: Selected readings. New York: Family Service Association of America, 1965, Pp. 202-219.

Kalis, B., Harris, M. R., Prestwood, A. R., and Freeman, E. Precipitating stress as a focus in psychotherapy, Archives of General Psychiatry, 1961, 5(3), 219-228.

Kaplan, D. M. A concept of acute situational disorder, Social Work, 1962, 7(2), 15-23.

Kaplan, D. M. Observations on crisis theory and practice, Social Casework, 1968, 49(3), 151-155.

Kaplan, D. M., and Mason, E. A. Maternal reactions to premature birth viewed as an acute emotional disorder, American Journal of Orthopsychiatry, 1960, 30(3), 539-552.

Karp, H. N., and Karls, J. M. Combining crisis therapy and mental health consultation, Archives of General Psychiatry, 1966, 14(5), 536-542.

Keith-Lucas, A. Structures in traditional agencies for crisis intervention, Child Welfare, 1969, 48(7), 420-422.

Kellner, R. Outlines of management of common psychiatric crises and
emergencies in the community, Psychosomatics, 1971, 12(3),
191-199.

Kirshner, L. A., and Kaplan, N. Conversion as a manifestation of crisis
in the life situation: A report of seven cases of ataxia and
paralysis of the lower extremities, Comprehensive Psychiatry,
1970, 11(3), 260-266.

Klein, D. C., and Lindemann, E. Preventive intervention in individual
and family crisis situations. In G. Caplan (Ed.) Prevention
of mental disorders in children: Initial exploration. New York:
Basic Books, 1961, Pp. 283-306.

Klein, D. C., and Ross, A. Kindergarten entry: A study of role
transition. In H. J. Parad (Ed.) Crisis intervention: Selected
readings. New York: Family Service Association of America,
1965, Pp. 140-148.

Klemme, H. L. Mid-life crisis, Menninger Perspective, 1970, 1(2), 2-6.

Koos, E. L. Class differences in family reactions to crisis, Marriage
and Family Living, 1950, 12(3), 77-78.

Koos, E. L. Dynamics of family interaction. New York: Duvall &
Hill, 1948.

Krause, E. A. On the time and place of crisis, Human Organization,
1968, 27(2), 110-116.

Krider, J. W. Desensitizing and resensitizing the schizogenic family
system, Social Casework, 1971, 52(6), 370-376.

Kritzer, H., and Pittman, F. S. Overnight psychiatric care in a general-
hospital emergency room, Hospital and Community Psychiatry, 1968,
19(10), 303-306.

Lamb, C. W. Telephone therapy: Some common errors and fallacies,
Voices: The Art and Science of Psychotherapy, 1969-1970,
5(4), 42-46.

Lang, P. A., and Oppenheimer, J. R. The influence of social work
when parents are faced with the fatal illness of a child,
Social Casework, 1968, 49(3), 161-166.

Langsley, D. G. Crisis intervention, American Journal of Psychiatry,
1972, 129(6), 734-736.

Langsley, D., et. al. Family crisis therapy -- Results and implications, Family Process, 1968, 7(2), 145-158. (a)

Langsley, D., et. al. Followup evaluation of family crisis therapy, American Journal of Orthopsychiatry, 1969, 39(5), 753-759.

Langsley, D. G., and Kaplan, D. M. The treatment of families in crisis. New York: Grune and Stratton, 1968. (b)

Langsley, D. G., Mackotha, P., and Flomenhaft, K. Avoiding mental hospital admission: A followup study, American Journal of Psychiatry, 1971, 127(10), 1391-1394.

LaSor, B., and Strickler, M. The concept of loss in crisis intervention, Mental Hygiene, 1970, 54(2), 301-305.

Lehamann, H. E. Stress dynamics in psychiatric perspective, Psychiatry, 1952, 15, 387-393.

Le Masters, E. E. Parenthood as crisis, Marriage and Family Living, 1957, 19(4), 352-355.

Lester, D. Attitudes toward death held by staff of a suicide prevention center, Psychological Reports, 1971, 28(2), 650. (a)

Lester, D. The evaluation of suicide prevention centers, International Behavioral Scientist, 1971, 3, 40-47. (b)

Lester, D. Geographical location of callers to a suicide prevention center: Note on the evaluation of suicide prevention programs, Psychological Reports, 1971, 28(2), 421-422. (c)

Lester, D. Recruitment of a counselor, Crisis Intervention, 1970, 2(2, Suppl.), 34-37. (a)

Lester, D. Steps toward the evaluation of a suicide prevention center: I, Crisis Intervention, 1970, 2(2, Suppl.), 42-45. (b)

Lester, D. Steps toward the evaluation of a suicide prevention center: II, Crisis Intervention, 1970, 2(1, Suppl.), 12-18. (c)

Lester, D. Steps toward the evaluation of a suicide prevention center: III, Crisis Intervention, 1970, 2(1, Suppl.), 19-21. (d)

Lester, D. Steps toward the evaluation of a suicide prevention center: IV, Crisis Intervention, 1970, 2(4), 20-22. (e)

Lester, D., and Williams, T. The volunteer in suicide prevention, Crisis Intervention, 1971, 3(4), 87-91. (d)

Lewis, W. W. Child advocacy and ecological planning, Mental Hygiene, 1970, 54(4), 475-483.

Lindemann, E. The meaning of crisis in individual and family living, Teachers College Record, 1956, 57(5), 310-315.

Lindemann, E. Symptomology and management of acute grief, American Journal of Psychiatry, 1944, 101(September), 141-148.

Lindenthal, J. J., Meyers, J. K., et. al. Mental status and religious behavior, Journal of the Scientific Study of Religion, 1970, 9(2), 143-149.

Lindenthal, J. J., Thomas, C. S., and Myers, J. K. Psychological status and the perception of primary and secondary support from the social milieu in time of crisis, Journal of Nervous and Mental Disease, 1971, 153(2), 92-98.

Litman, R. E. Suicide prevention center patients: A followup study, Bulletin of Suicidology, 1970, 6(Spring), 12-17.

Lucas, R. A. Men in crisis. New York: Basic Books, 1969.

Lundberg, C. C. Managerial behavior in a crisis, Personnel Journal, 1970, 49(10), 847-860.

Mackey, R. A. Crisis theory: Its development and relevance to casework practice, Family Coordinator, 1968, 17(3), 165-173.

Madison, P. The campus: Coming of age at college, Psychology Today, 1971, 5(5), 73-74, 104-106.

Malamud, W. Adaptation and growth, Mental Hygiene, 1927, 11, 584-598.

Malecki, J. J. Life history approach to the study of crises in religious life, Dissertation Abstracts International, 1970, 30(12-B), 5693.

McGee, R. K. The suicide prevention center as a model for community mental health programs, Community Mental Health Journal, 1965, 1(2), 162-170.

McGee, T. F. Some basic considerations in crisis intervention, Community Mental Health Journal, 1968, 4(4), 319-325.

Menninger, K. A. Psychological aspects of the organism under stress, Journal of American Psychoanalytic Association, 1954, 2, 280-310.

Mikawa, J. K. A university affliated suicide prevention center, Crisis Intervention, 1971, 3(1), 3-7.

Miller, K., and Iscoe, I. The concept of crisis: Current status and mental health implications, Human Organization, 1963, 22(3), 195-201.

Miller, L. C. Short-term therapy with adolescents. In H. J. Parad (Ed.) Crisis intervention: Selected readings. New York: Family Service Association of America, 1965, Pp. 157-166.

Moore, H. E. Tornadoes over texas: A study of waco and san angelo in disaster. Austin, Texas: University Press, 1958.

Morley, W. E. Theory of crisis intervention, Pastoral Psychology, 1970, 21(203), 14-20.

Morley, W. E., and Brown, V. The crisis-intervention group: A natural mating or a marriage of convenience? Psychotherapy, 1969, 6(1), 30-36.

Morrissey, J. R. Death anxiety in children with a fatal illness, American Journal of Psychotherapy, 1964, 27(4), 606-615.

Munoz, R. A., Tuason, V. B., and Dick, E. Psychiatric emergency room service patterns, Comprehensive Psychiatry, 1970, 11(2), 185-189.

Murphy, G. E., et. al. Who calls the suicide prevention center: A study of 55 persons calling on their own behalf, American Journal of Psychiatry, 1969, 126(3), 314-324.

Murphy, J. G. A comparative analysis of the attitudes of socio-economically deprived clients toward two treatment modalities, Dissertation Abstracts International, 1970, 31(6-A), 3048.

Musgrave, L. C. Hot line takes the heat off, American Journal of Nursing, 1971, 71(4), 756-759.

Myers, J. K., Lindenthal, J. J., and Pepper, M. P. Life events and psychiatric impairment, Journal of Nervous and Mental Disease, 1971, 152(3), 149-157.

Nolfi, M. W. Family in grief: The question of casework intervention, Social Work, 1967, 12(4), 40-46.

Noyes, R. Shall we prevent suicide? Comprehensive Psychiatry, 1970, 11(4), 361-370.

Nuckolls, K. B. Psychosocial assests, life crises and the prognosis of pregnancy, Dissertation Abstracts International, 1970, 31(5-B), 2796.

Oberleder, M. Crisis therapy in mental breakdown of the aging, The Gerontologist, 1970, 10(2), 111-114.

Oetting, E. R., Cole, C. W., and Adams, R. Problems in program evaluation: A ministers' workshop, Mental Hygiene, 1969, 53(2), 214-217.

Oppenheimer, J. R. Use of crisis intervention in casework with the cancer patient and his family, Social Work, 1967, 12(2), 44-52.

Parad, H. J. Crisis intervention, Encyclopedia of social work. (16th ed.) Vol. 1. New York: National Association of Social Workers, 1971.

Parad, H. J. (Ed.) Crisis intervention: Selected readings. New York: Family Service Association of America, 1965. (a)

Parad, H. J. Preventive casework: Problems and implications. In H. J. Parad (Ed.) Crisis intervention: Selected readings. New York: Family Service Association of America, 1965, Pp. 284-302. (b)

Parad, H. J. The use of time-limited crisis intervention in community mental health programming, Social Service Review, 1966, 40(3), 275-282.

Parad, H. J., and Caplan, G. A. Framework for studying families in crisis, Social Work, 1960, 5(3), 3-15.

Parad, H. J., and Parad, L. A study of crisis-oriented planned short-term treatment: Part I and part II, Social Casework, 1968, 49(6-7), 346-355, 418-426.

Parsons, B. V. Family crisis intervention: Therapy outcome study, Dissertation Abstracts International, 1972, 32(11-B), 6657.

Pasewark, R. A., and Albers, D. A. Crisis intervention: Theory in search of a program, Social Work, 1972, 17(2), 70-77.

Paul, L. Crisis intervention, Mental Hygiene, 1966, 50(1), 141-145. (a)

Paul, L. Treatment techniques in a walk-in-clinic, Hospital and Community Psychiatry, 1966, 17(2), 49-51. (b)

Peck, H. B., and Kaplan, S. Crisis theory and therapeutic change in small groups: Some implications for community mental health programs, International Journal of Group Psychotherapy, 1966, 16(2), 135-149.

Perlman, H. H. Some notes on the waiting list, Social Casework, 1963, 44(4), 200-205.

Polak, P. The crisis of admission, Social Psychiatry, 1967, 2(4), 150-157.

Pollack, D. Crisis and response in college students, Journal of Abnormal Psychology, 1971, 78(1), 49-51.

Porter, R. A. Crisis intervention and social work models, Community Mental Health Journal, 1966, 2(1), 13-21.

Pretzel, P. W. The role of the clergyman in suicide prevention, Pastoral Psychology, 1970, 21(203), 47-52. (a)

Pretzel, P. W. The volunteer clinical worker at the suicide prevention center, Bulletin of Suicidology, 1970, 6(Spring), 29-34. (b)

Prevention of suicide, Public Health Papers, 1968, No. 35.

Quinby, S. V., and Berstein, N. R. How children live after disfiguring burns, Psychiatry in Medicine, 1971, 2(2), 146-159.

Raphling, D. L., and Lion, J. Patients with repeated admissions to a psychiatric emergency service, Community Mental Health Journal, 1970, 6(4), 313-318.

Rapoport, L. Crisis intervention as a mode of brief treatment. In R. W. Roberts and R. H. Nee (Eds.) Theories of social casework. Chicago: The University of Chicago Press, 1970, Pp. 265-312.

Rapoport, L. Crisis-oriented short-term casework, Social Service Review, 1967, 41(1), 31-43.

Rapoport, L. The state of crisis: Some theoretical considerations, Social Service Review, 1962, 36(2), 211-217. (a)

Rapoport, L. Working with families in crisis: An exploration in preventive intervention, Social Work, 1962, 7(3), 48-56. (b)

Rapoport, R. V. Normal crisis, family structure and mental health, Family Process, 1963, 2(1), 68-80.

Rhine, M. W., and Mayerson, P. Crisis hospitalization within a psychiatric emergency service, American Journal of Psychiatry, 1971, 127(10), 1386-1391.

Richman, J., and Davidoff, I. F. Interaction testing and counseling as a form of crisis intervention during marital therapy, Proceedings of the Convention of the American Psychological Association, 1971, 6(1), 439-440.

Riscalla, L. M. Crisis therapy with adolescents, International Journal of Offender Therapy, 1970, 14(1), 40-43.

Ritchie, A. Multiple impact therapy: An experiment. In H. J. Parad (Ed.) Crisis intervention: Selected readings. New York: Family Service Association of America, 1965, Pp. 227-236.

Roberts, R. W., and Nee, R. H. (Eds.) Theories of social casework. Chicago: The University of Chicago Press, 1970.

Robinson, M. Family reaction to stress, Medical Social Work, 1968, 22(6), 191-199.

Rogers, C. G. The use of alienation in crisis work, Journal of Psychiatric Nursing and Mental Health Services, 1970, 8(6), 7-11.

Rogers, W. F. Needs of the bereaved, Pastoral Psychology, 1950, 1(5), 17-21.

Rosenbaum, M. Emotional aspects of wartime separations, The Family, 1944, 24(9), 337-341.

Rosenfeld, J. M., and Caplan, G. Techniques of staff consultation in an immigrant children's organization, American Journal of Orthopsychiatry, 1954, 24(1), 42-62.

Rosner, J. Crisis and support in therapy with children, American Journal of Orthopsychiatry, 1959, 2(1), 144-156.

Rubinstein, D. Rehospitalization versus family crisis intervention, American Journal of Psychiatry, 1972, 129(6), 715-720.

Rusk, T. N. Opportunity and technique in crisis psychiatry, Comprehensive Psychiatry, 1971, 12(3), 249-263.

Rusk, T. N., and Gerner, R. H. A study of the process of emergency psychotherapy, American Journal of Psychiatry, 1972, 128(7), 882-886.

Sachs, V. K. Crisis intervention, Public Welfare, 1968, 26(2), 112-117.

Satloff, A., and Worby, C. M. The psychiatric emergency service: Mirror of change, American Journal of Psychiatry, 1970, 126(11), 1628-1632.

Schulberg, H. C., and Sheldon, A. The probability of crisis and strategies for preventive intervention, Archives of General Psychiatry, 1968, 18(5), 553-558.

Schulman, R. Suicide prevention and the volunteer, Menninger Perspective, 1972, 3(3), 15-18.

Schwartz, D. A., Weiss, A. T., and Miner, J. M. Community psychiatry and emergency service, American Journal of Psychiatry, 1972, 129(6), 710-715.

Selltiz, C., Jahoda, M., Deutsch, M., and Cook, S. W. Research methods in social relations. New York: Holt, Rinehart and Winston, 1959.

Senay, E. C. Therapeutic abortion: Clinical aspects, Archives of General Psychiatry, 1970, 23(5), 408-415.

Shields, L. Family crisis intervention, Journal of Psychiatric Nursing and Mental Health Services, 1969, 7(5), 222-225.

Sifneos, P. A. A concept of "emotional crisis", Mental Hygiene, 1960, 44(2), 169-179.

Signell, K. A. The crisis of unwed motherhood: A consultation approach, Community Mental Health Journal, 1969, 5(4), 304-313.

Smith, R. E. Changes in locus of control as a function of life crisis resolution, Journal of Abnormal Psychology, 1970, 75(3), 319-332.

Sokolow, L., et. al. The effect of distribution of information about crisis intervention services on number of calls to a suicide prevention center, Crisis Intervention, 1971, 3(4), 91-92.

Speer, D. C. Rate of caller re-use of a telephone crisis service, Crisis Intervention, 1971, 3(4), 83-86.

Spilken, A. Z., and Jacobs, M. A. Prediction of illness behavior from measures of life crisis, manifest distress and maladaptive coping, Psychosomatic Medicine, 1971, 33(3), 251-264.

Stein, C. Practical pastoral counseling. Springfield, Illnois: Charles C. Thomas, 1970.

Stein, K. M. A challenge to the role of the crisis concept in emergency psychotherapy, Dissertation Abstracts International, 1970, 30 (11-B), 5245.

Stein, M. The function of ambiguity in child crises, Journal of the American Academy of Child Psychiatry, 1970, 9(3), 462-476.

Strickler, M. Applying crisis theory in a community clinic, Social Casework, 1965, 46(3), 150-154.

Strickler, M., and Allgeyer, J. The crisis group: A new application of crisis theory, Social Work, 1967, 12(3), 28-32.

Strumpfer, D. J. Fear and affliation during a disaster, Journal of Social Psychology, 1970, 82(2), 263-268.

Strunk, O., and Jordan, M. R. An experimental course for clergymen in suicidology and crisis intervention, Journal of Pastoral Care, 1972, 26(1), 50-54.

Stubblebine, J. M., and Decker, J. B. Are urban mental health centers worth it? American Journal of Psychiatry, 1971, 128(4), 480-483.

Sutherland, S., and Scherl, D. J. Patterns of response among victims of rape, American Journal of Orthopsychiatry, 1970, 40(3), 503-511.

Switzer, D. K. Crisis intervention techniques for the minister, Pastoral Psychology, 1970, 21(203), 29-36.

Sze, W. C. A study of the effect of social variables on psychiatric emergency situations among children, Dissertation Abstracts International, 1970, 31(1-A), 475.

Tabacknick, N., and Klugman, D. Anonymous suicidal telephone calls: A research critique, Psychiatry, 1970, 33(4), 526-532.

Taplin, J. R. Crisis theory: Critique and reformation, Community Mental Health Journal, 1971, 7(1), 13-23.

Torop, P., and Torop, K. Hotlines and youth culture values, American Journal of Psychiatry, 1972, 129(6), 730-733.

Turner, R. J. Social structure and crisis: A study of nursing organization and patient adjustment, Community Mental Health Journal, 1966, 2(4), 285-292.

Ungerleider, J. T. The psychiatric emergency, Archives of General Psychiatry, 1960, 3(6), 593-601.

Vernick, J. The use of the life space interview on a medical ward. In H. J. Parad (Ed.) Crisis intervention: Selected readings. New York: Family Service Association of America, 1965, Pp. 149-156.

Villeponteaux, L. Crisis intervention in day school for delinquents, Crime and Delinquency, 1970, 16(3), 317-323.

Vincent, R. G. Therapeutic intervention with children in small groups: A review and conceptualization of research gaps and the development of teaching modules. Unpublished doctoral dissertation, University of Utah, Graduate School of Social Work, June, 1972.

Vosburg, R. L. Disaster alert and the community mental health center, Community Mental Health Journal, 1971, 7(1), 24-28.

Waldfogel, S., and Gardner, G. E. Intervention in crisis as a method of primary prevention. In G. Caplan (Ed.) The prevention of mental disorder in children: Initial exploration. New York: Basic Books, 1961, Pp. 307-322.

Waldman, M. Psychodynamics and educational orientation in the special school, Reading Teacher, 1970, 23(4), 325-330, 359.

Walton, M., Reeves, G. D., and Shannon, R. F. Crisis team intervention in school-community unrest, Social Casework, 1971, 52(1), 11-17.

Waltzer, H., and Hankoff, L. D. One year's experience with a suicide prevention telephone service, Community Mental Health Journal, 1965, 1(4), 309-315.

Whitlock, G. E. The pastor's use of crisis intervention, Pastoral Psychology, 1970, 21(203), 37-46.

Wolberg, L. R. Short-term psychotherapy. New York: Grune & Stratton, 1965.

Yasser, A. M. Treating the bad trip by telephone, Crisis Intervention, 1970, 2(1, Suppl.), 25-26.